NEXT LEVEL
BUSINESS
MINDSET

LEARNING LEADERSHIP ACT AND THE WAY OF SUCCESSFUL PEOPLE

Dr. JORDAN RILEY

DISCLAIMER

The information provided in this book is for general informational purposes only. It is meant as a complement to enhance the reader's understanding.

- <u>CONTINUES LEARNING AND IMPROVEMENT</u>

BUILDING A STRONG TEAM
- <u>RECRUITING THE RIGHT PEOPLE</u>
- <u>FOSTERING A POSITIVE TEAM CULTURE</u>
- <u>EFFECTIVE TEAM COMMUNICATION</u>
- <u>CONFLICT RESOLUTION STRATEGIES</u>

<u>Conclusion</u>

INTRODUCTION

"Great leaders are created, not born. And they are created with laborious effort, just like anything else.
-"Vince Lombardi"

"Leadership's highest calling is to facilitate people's growth and development.
-"Harvey S. Firestone"

"Creating more leaders rather than followers is the goal of leadership.
-"Ralph Nader"

Picture yourself standing on the brink of a huge ocean, with an infinite horizon in front of you. The water is a metaphor for the limitless possibilities and difficulties found in the corporate world, where each wave and current reflects the dynamically shifting nature of strategy, leadership, and innovation. The correct attitude and abilities serve as your compass as you get ready to dive in, leading you to undiscovered success hotspots. Your navigational guide, "Next Level Business Mindset: Learning Leadership Act and the Way of Successful People," provides you with the knowledge and techniques you need to become an expert leader in the complicated and ever-changing world of today.

The old methods are no longer adequate in today's corporate world. A new kind of leader is required due to the quick speed of technical improvements, the worldwide interconnection of markets, and the changing expectations of both customers and staff. Someone who not only knows how to manage resources well but also how to stimulate creativity, build teamwork, and promote ongoing progress. This book serves as a road map for those who want to go above and beyond the norm, lead with intention, and develop an outlook that transforms setbacks into learning opportunities.

You'll go on a life-changing adventure from the first page, delving into the depths of what it means to cultivate a business attitude that goes beyond profit and loss statements. You'll learn how to develop a growth-oriented viewpoint—one that welcomes change and finds strength in difficulties. You will acquire a more profound comprehension of the fundamental characteristics that set exceptional leaders apart from the others by examining real-life scenarios and pragmatic perspectives. Whether you are an experienced CEO, an aspiring business owner, or a team leader, the concepts and tactics in this book are meant to push your ideas and behavior to the next level.

The idea of a business mindset—a proactive, purposeful, and resilient way of thinking—lays the foundation for this journey. It involves gaining a broad perspective, spotting patterns, and setting up your business and yourself for long-term success. This way of thinking changes with every encounter, every insight gained, and every obstacle surmounted. It serves as the cornerstone upon which all other leadership attributes are constructed, offering the assurance and clarity required to successfully negotiate the intricacies of the corporate world.

As these chapters demonstrate, leadership is more than just jobs and titles. It all comes down to vision, influence, and motivating others to work together toward common objectives. You will explore the attributes of a genuinely effective leader, including communication abilities, emotional intelligence, decision-making, and problem-solving capabilities. These qualities are talents that can be acquired and refined via deliberate effort and self-awareness rather than being innate qualities. Your team and organization will benefit from your understanding and cultivation of these traits, which will promote success and an excellence-oriented culture.

Another important topic covered in this book is the difference between management and leadership. Even though they are both necessary, they call for distinct strategies and perspectives. Keeping things in order, making sure things run smoothly, and achieving goals are all parts of management. In contrast, leadership entails guiding change, encouraging people, and creating a vision. This book will assist you in comprehending how to successfully strike a balance between these jobs and utilize each one's advantages to build an agile and adaptable company.

You will also discover the vital role that emotional intelligence plays in leadership as you go through these pages. The capacity to comprehend and control emotions, both your own and those of others, is a critical difference in a time when interpersonal interactions and human connections are valued highly. A more unified and driven team can be produced by utilizing emotional intelligence to improve communication, trust-building, and conflict resolution skills. This book offers doable methods for enhancing emotional intelligence, giving you the ability to lead with sincerity and empathy.

Any successful organization needs effective communication to function. Leaders establish a culture of transparency and trust, resolve problems, and align their teams through compassionate, succinct, and clear communication. This book explores the subtleties of communication skills, including strategies and ideas to support you in sharing your ideas, giving helpful criticism, and engaging in active listening. Gaining proficiency in these abilities will help you improve teamwork and lead your group to success as a whole.

Making decisions and solving problems are fundamental to being a leader. In the current dynamic and intricate corporate landscape, executives need to possess the ability to promptly and efficiently make well-informed decisions. This book delves into the nuances of these abilities, offering frameworks and tactics to support your scenario analysis, choice evaluation, and solution implementation. You can lead your business with confidence and navigate uncertainty by improving your decision-making and problem-solving skills.

Developing presence and confidence is another essential component of good leadership. Possessing confidence gives you credibility and trust, while confidence helps you demand attention and project authority. These qualities can be acquired via introspection, training, and a dedication to ongoing development. This book provides strategies and insights to help you develop your presence and confidence so you can lead with assurance and effect.

Achieving the status of a next-level leader is a collaborative process. It entails interacting with people, picking up knowledge from their experiences, and never stopping trying to get better. By examining the authentic case studies and useful illustrations in this book, you will get important knowledge about how effective leaders overcome obstacles, motivate their groups, and accomplish their objectives. These anecdotes demonstrate the influence of a growth mindset and capable leadership on the accomplishment of organizational goals.

As you set out on this path, keep in mind that being a leader is a continuous process that requires learning, adapting, and developing. This book's chapters each provide a piece of the puzzle, assisting you in developing a thorough grasp of the skills required to lead in the intricate and ever-changing corporate world of today. Through the adoption of the ideas and methods shown in these pages, you may develop a cutting-edge business mindset and develop into the kind of leader who motivates people and creates long-term success. There is an ocean of opportunity waiting for you; seize it and find your path to success.

CHAPTER 1

UNDERSTANDING THE BUSINESS MINDSET

"Work, discipline, and training are essential for success in the corporate world. However, if you don't let these problems scare you, the opportunities are as good as they've ever been."

-*"DAVID ROCKEFELLER"*

"Effective corporate leaders have a clear vision, communicate it effectively, embrace it wholeheartedly, and work tirelessly to see it through to completion."

-*"JACK WELCH"*

WHAT IS A BUSINESS MINDSET?

Every successful CEO, business leader, or entrepreneur possesses the vital, frequently intangible trait known as the business mindset. This kind of thinking sets visionaries who create industries apart from those who just work in them. But what really is a business mindset, and how does it work to propel achievement? Gaining a knowledge of this idea is like trying to piece together a complicated tapestry, where each piece—whether it is resilience, vision, or adaptability—interweaves to form a dynamic and cohesive whole.

In order to fully understand the nature of a business mindset, we must first acknowledge that it is a specific style of thinking and seeing the world rather than just knowledge or abilities. This way of thinking captures how people approach problems, decide what to do, and communicate with others. It is based on the capacity to turn chances into real accomplishments by seeing them where others see barriers.

Imagine yourself strolling through a busy marketplace where sellers are yelling at passersby and the aroma of spices and fresh produce fills the air. A person with a business perspective sees opportunities and patterns in the midst of turmoil. They take note of the most popular stalls, eye-catching product arrangements, and the ebb and flow of market dynamics. This person can see the bigger picture of how the market functions and how it can be maximized, not just the immediate transactions. The foundation of the business mindset is this larger picture.

The narrative of Sara Blakely, the creator of Spanx, serves as an instructive example of this way of thinking. Blakely spotted a business opportunity instead of just an annoyance when she saw the uncomfortable and ugly appearance of traditional hosiery. She was able to conceive a product that could completely transform the undergarment business because to her thinking. Her steadfast faith in her vision and her unrelenting pursuit of innovation led to the establishment of a billion-dollar empire despite multiple rejections and obstacles. Blakely's journey highlights the significance of having a business mindset, which is defined by seeing beyond the present to the prospective future.

Resilience and the capacity to see and seize future opportunities are related. The ability to bounce back from setbacks and disappointments is crucial in the corporate sector, where people must possess resilience to get through rough patches. Understanding that failure is merely a stage on the way to success rather than the end is a component of a business mindset. The well-known words of Thomas Edison, "I have not failed. "I've discovered 10,000 methods that are ineffective," perfectly captures this tenacity. The business approach is exemplified by Edison's unwavering experimenting and determination to let failure deter him. They show an attitude that sees failure not as a final setback but as a chance for growth and learning.

Resilience by itself, though, is insufficient. Additionally, a business attitude necessitates a never-ending need for knowledge and flexibility. Technology developments, consumer behavior, and changes in the socioeconomic landscape all impact how businesses operate today. People that have a business perspective welcome this shift, continuously looking to learn new things and modifying their approaches accordingly. They know that progress is hampered by complacency. Businesses such as Amazon, which constantly innovates and enters new markets, exhibit this kind of thinking. The creator of Amazon, Jeff Bezos, is well known for emphasizing the value of being "stubborn on vision and flexible on details." This attitude captures the difficult balance that lies at the core of the business mindset: the ability to adjust to changing circumstances while remaining steadfastly committed to a long-term vision.

Interpersonal interactions are a critical component that is intricately linked to vision, resilience, and adaptation. People are at the core of business: partners, stakeholders, employees, and consumers. A business mindset is having a keen understanding of these connections and knowing how to handle them. Important elements include empathy, emotional intelligence, and effective communication. Through their relationships, successful corporate leaders inspire loyalty and foster trust. They know that building strong networks and cultivating a positive company culture can have a big impact on how successful their business is. Leaders such as Howard Schultz of Starbucks, who stressed the creation of a "third place" between home and work by cultivating a sense of community and connection within his cafés, are prime examples of this relational aspect of the business approach.

Additionally, having a strong sense of ethics and integrity is essential to having a business perspective. Upholding moral principles is crucial in a time when corporate crises have the power to destroy firms and weaken public confidence. A moral compass helps leaders with a business perspective make sure their actions are consistent with their beliefs and ideals. They know that credibility and trust are the cornerstones of long-term success. This ethical dimension involves actively promoting the welfare of society and the environment in addition to abstaining from wrongdoing. Businesses that include environmental sustainability in their operations, such as Patagonia, are prime examples of this dedication. Their success shows that profitable operations and moral business conduct don't have to conflict; in fact, they can strengthen one another.

As we integrate vision, adaptability, resilience, interpersonal skills, and ethics, the business mindset's intricate fabric starts to take shape. It is a dynamic and multidimensional method of thinking that helps people to lead innovation and growth while navigating the difficulties of the commercial environment. It is a constant process of growth and improvement rather than a fixed quality.

Let's look at Elon Musk's story to get a better idea of the scope and depth of the business approach. Musk's endeavors, ranging from PayPal to SpaceX and Tesla, demonstrate an unwavering concentration on revolutionary ideas. He is relentless in his pursuit of possibilities that most would write off as science fiction. Musk's approach to business is distinguished by his willingness to take enormous risks, his ability to bounce back from setbacks, and his flexibility in changing course when called for. His management approach also emphasizes how critical it is to assemble a solid team and motivate them to embrace his vision. Musk's tale serves as evidence of the tremendous success that can be attained with a commercial perspective.

But it's crucial to understand that not all prominent CEOs and entrepreneurs have the same business approach. It applies to people in every field and at every organizational level equally. Developing a business attitude may help anyone, whether they are a manager, small business owner, or entry-level employee, be more successful and fulfilled. It entails going into one's work with a purpose, being dedicated to ongoing progress, and being open to change and innovation.

Take a middle management at a manufacturing company, for example. This manager can spot inefficiencies in production processes and lead efforts to change them by embracing a business attitude. They can encourage a cooperative team atmosphere where workers are inspired to give their all and feel appreciated. They can adopt new technologies to increase production and stay up to date on market trends. By doing this, they improve not just their own professional opportunities but also the company's overall success.

Beyond the office, developing a commercial attitude has consequences. It can improve a person's quality of life by encouraging traits like adaptation, resilience, and taking the initiative to overcome obstacles. It promotes a growth-oriented viewpoint, in which people view every circumstance as an opportunity for personal progress and learning. Positivity can result in increased self-worth and a feeling of authority.

When one looks back on the process of learning about the business mindset, it is evident that it is a mindset that can be fostered and developed rather than an elusive quality held by a few number of people. It calls for the ability to go outside of one's comfort zone, accept uncertainty, and persevere in the face of difficulty. It entails a dedication to moral values and an understanding of how society and business are intertwined.

Further investigation reveals that the corporate perspective is fundamentally forward-looking. It involves seeing a better future and acting proactively to bring that vision to pass. It's about becoming a change agent—someone who initiates change rather than just reacts to it. This forward-looking viewpoint is essential in a world where change is happening faster than ever before and the problems we face are getting more complicated.

To sum up, the business mindset is a complex and dynamic way of thinking that includes ethics, vision, resilience, and flexibility in addition to interpersonal abilities. It helps people to generate innovation and growth, succeed sustainably, and negotiate the intricacies of the business environment. It is a constant process of growth and improvement rather than a fixed quality. Cultivating a business mindset can result in increased performance, fulfillment, and impact for anyone involved in the business world—whether they are employees, entrepreneurs, or leaders. It is the vision that propels advancement, the fortitude that maintains resilience, and the spark that sparks creativity. The business mindset is the compass that points people in the direction of their dreams and aspirations in the ever-changing world of business, turning them into realities.

IMPORTANCE OF GROWTH MINDSET

The idea that you can improve your skills via perseverance, wise planning, and advice from others is known as a growth mindset.

*-"**CAROL DWECK**"*

"You are correct, regardless of whether you believe you can or cannot."

*-"**HENRY FORD**"*

The idea of a growth mentality has become extremely important in the modern world, where difficulties appear at every turn and change is the only constant. A growth mindset, as defined by psychologist Carol Dweck, is the conviction that aptitude and intelligence can be enhanced with commitment, diligence, and appropriate techniques. This viewpoint contrasts sharply with a fixed mindset, which holds that aptitudes are inherent and unalterable. It is essential to comprehend and adopt a growth mindset not only for personal development but also for success in relationships, education, the workplace, and almost every aspect of life.

Take Sarah's experience as an example. She was raised in a small town with little chances and traditional assumptions that frequently shaped her life. Sarah had never excelled in any area and had always been an ordinary student. She had been subtly told by her family, professors, and community that she was just "not cut out for" high academic or professional success. On the other hand, Sarah had a strong desire to fulfill her potential and a modest curiosity about the world outside of her local surroundings.

Sarah first learned about the idea of a development mindset at a conference she attended in her senior year of high school. The speaker gave motivational tales of people who had changed their life by being persistent and open to taking advice from their mistakes. This was a revelation to Sarah. She came to see that her perceived limitations were more the result of an embedded mindset than of her actual capabilities.

Equipped with this fresh viewpoint, Sarah made the decision to push herself. She had a newfound feeling of purpose for her studies and approached challenging courses with the conviction that hard work and perseverance will pay off. There were numerous moments of doubt and irritation, and the results did not come right away. But every tiny victory, every idea grasped, strengthened her faith in her ability to advance. She started to view setbacks as chances to improve rather than as evidence of her shortcomings.

Sarah experienced significant effects on her academic achievement and self-esteem from this mental transformation. She had risen to the top of her class by the time she graduated, winning a scholarship to a prominent institution. More significantly, though, was that Sarah had acquired a lifelong love of study and resilience.

Sarah's growth mentality helped her advance when she was in college. She had always been attracted by engineering, but had previously thought it would be too difficult, so she decided to pursue it. There was a lot of competition and challenging coursework. Sarah had a hard time at first keeping up because many of her peers had come from backgrounds with more demanding academic preparation. Still, she persevered, keeping in mind the development mindset's tenets. She worked with classmates, asked teachers for assistance, and committed herself to learning the subject. Her efforts eventually paid off. She not only did exceptionally well in her classes, but she also started to participate in innovation and research projects.

Sarah's story demonstrates the growth mindset's capacity for transformation. She reached potential she had never dreamed of by accepting difficulties and having faith in her abilities to go better. Her experience serves as a microcosm of the larger effects that growth mindsets may have on people and businesses.

The field of entrepreneurship is arguably where the value of a growth mindset in the workplace is most apparent. Innovative and startup businesses frequently work in unpredictably changing contexts. To succeed in these kinds of situations, one must be willing to try new things, take calculated chances, and learn from mistakes. Employees that have a growth mindset are more likely to work in an environment where innovation is encouraged and failures are viewed as necessary parts of the learning process.

Consider the tale of Elon Musk and SpaceX, for example. Many people thought Musk's plan to lower the cost of space travel and eventually allow for human colonization of Mars was unrealistic. Numerous difficulties and well-publicized mishaps, such as several rocket explosions, beset SpaceX. But SpaceX's final success was largely due to Musk's iterative improvement philosophy and his persistent dedication to picking up lessons from every setback. The company's growth mindset-based culture inspired engineers to keep going after failures, which resulted in ground-breaking space exploration accomplishments.

In schooling, a growth attitude is equally important. Educators that follow this methodology inspire their pupils to rise to difficulties and see hard work as a means of becoming proficient. This has significant effects on the motivation and performance of students. Students are more likely to engage deeply in their learning, persevere through challenges, and perform at greater levels when they believe that their abilities can be developed. According to research, students who adopt a growth mindset are more adaptable, more eager to take on difficult assignments, and more successful in their academic pursuits.

A growth mindset also encourages lifelong learning, which is an essential quality in a world that is changing quickly. The information and abilities necessary for success now can become outdated tomorrow. People that have a growth mindset are more capable of adapting, learning new abilities, and maintaining their relevance in the workforce. The need of this adaptability is growing as globalization and technology breakthroughs change markets for jobs and sectors.

Additionally transformational is a developing perspective in interpersonal interactions. It encourages people to approach disagreements and difficulties with an open mind and a desire to learn and develop. A development mentality sees relationships as dynamic and ever-evolving, as opposed to fixed entities. Relationships that are healthier and more resilient are those in which both partners are dedicated to mutual support and ongoing progress.

It is important to consider the effects of a growth mindset on one's own health and wellbeing. According to studies, people who have a growth mindset are more likely to adopt healthy habits, heal from illnesses more quickly, and keep their mental health in better shape. This is partially due to the fact that a growth mentality promotes initiative and perseverance in the face of difficulty.

Developing a growth mindset is a continuous process that calls for deliberate effort. It entails questioning one's own self-limiting ideas, asking for criticism, and being prepared to move outside one's comfort zone. It necessitates changing the emphasis from results to the process of growth and learning.

As one considers these concepts, it is evident that developing a development mindset involves more than just succeeding in the traditional sense. It is about adopting a lifestyle that prioritizes education, resiliency, and the never-ending quest of both professional and personal development. It's about realizing that potential is a quality that can be developed with hard work and persistence rather than a set attribute.

Take the life of Thomas Edison, one of the most successful inventors in history. Although Edison is well known for his numerous discoveries, his attitude toward failure is just as noteworthy. It is well known that before creating the workable electric lightbulb, Edison carried out thousands of trials. Edison allegedly said, "I have not failed," in response to a question regarding his frequent mistakes. Just now, I discovered 10,000 ineffective strategies. This viewpoint captures the spirit of a growth mindset. Edison's success was the product of constant testing, learning, and development rather than just natural brilliance.

In a similar vein, the accomplishments of sports figures such as Michael Jordan serve as prime examples of the value of a growth mindset. Throughout his career, Jordan—who is recognized as one of the best basketball players of all time—experienced many disappointments and defeats. He lost a lot of games, was benched from his high school basketball team, and missed a lot of shots. Nevertheless, Jordan saw every setback as a chance to get better. His unwavering dedication to progress and diligent work ethic enabled him to reach remarkable heights. Jordan's tale serves as an example of how excellence is the product of consistent work and a readiness to take lessons from every event rather than a predetermined quality.

A growth mentality is important for leadership as well. Leaders that adopt this perspective are better at encouraging and inspiring their groups. They establish settings that are supportive of people's personal development and foster an atmosphere where creativity flourishes. These leaders are aware that their job is to develop people's potential as well as to guide them. They regard personal growth as a continuous process and set an example for the habits they want to see in their teams.

On the other hand, CEOs who have a rigid mindset could hinder innovation and reduce the potential of their company. They foster circumstances where the fear of failure is prevalent by emphasizing the preservation of the status quo and avoiding risks. This lowers staff engagement and morale in addition to impeding creativity.

The field of social change is another area where a growth mentality is crucial. Those who are committed to bringing about change and who think that things can get better are more inclined to keep going after facing difficult obstacles. Their tenacity and dedication are fueled by their conviction that good things can happen. They realize that social advancement is a path that calls for constant work, education, and flexibility.

As we reflect on the significance of a growth mindset, it becomes evident that this idea is a framework for promoting resilience, creativity, and ongoing improvement in all facets of life rather than only a tool for personal success. It is a way of thinking that empowers us to believe in our ability to change and grow, to see opportunities where others perceive barriers, and to persevere in the face of difficulty.

In summary, the transforming capacity of a development mindset explains its significance. It serves as a motivator for both professional and personal growth, a base for resilience and creativity, and a tenet for effective leadership and constructive societal change. Adopting a growth mindset allows us to enter a world of possibilities where obstacles become learning opportunities, setbacks become experiences, and our potential is unbounded. A richer, more satisfying life and constant improvement are possible with a growth mindset, regardless of one's circumstances in life—be it relationships, business, education, or personal well-being.

CASE STUDIES: SUCCESSFUL BUSINESS MINDSET

The business world is replete with tales of astounding triumphs and setbacks, but what frequently sets the winners apart from the losers is not only the originality of a product or the genius of an idea, but also the mindset of people in charge. The components of a successful business attitude include vision, flexibility, resilience, and an unwavering dedication to learning. By examining case studies, we may acquire a more profound comprehension of how these components combine to propel exceptional accomplishments.

Think about Reed Hastings' and Netflix's journey. Hastings co-founded Netflix in the late 1990s as a DVD rental-by-mail business, an idea sparked by his annoyance at a late fee from a video rental company. As revolutionary as the concept was, it was Hastings' forward-thinking attitude and flexibility that really put Netflix on the map. In the early 2000s, Hastings predicted that digital content will overtake physical media as internet speed and streaming technology developed. He was far from complacent, even with their DVD rental business succeeding. He oversaw Netflix's large streaming investment, which at the time was a hazardous decision.

The company's content strategy, technology infrastructure, and business model all had to undergo substantial adjustments as a result of this strategic shift. Hastings is a prime example of the value of having a visionary mentality in business because of his forward-thinking outlook and his capacity to unite his staff around this new course. Under his direction, Netflix changed the entertainment landscape by going from a DVD rental service to a massive streaming platform and then producing its own original content. Netflix's long-term success has been largely attributed to its ability to adapt to changing market conditions and welcome change.

The narrative around Elon Musk and his businesses, especially Tesla and SpaceX, is another fascinating case study. Musk has a mindset defined by great vision and unwavering execution. At the time of Musk's founding of Tesla, most people considered electric cars to be a niche market with few people believing they could be widely adopted. But Musk saw an age in which electric cars (EVs) were not just practical, but desirable. His objective was to expedite the introduction of sustainable transportation by launching attractive mass-market electric vehicles as soon as feasible.

From manufacturing setbacks and problems with quality control to financial difficulties and mistrust from the auto industry and customers, Tesla's journey has not been without its share of difficulties. However, Musk's approach has proved essential to overcoming these challenges. His willingness to take significant risks, his ability to balance short-term crises with long-term goals, and his dedication to innovation have helped Tesla grow into one of the most valuable automakers in the world. Musk has a visionary yet persistently pragmatic worldview, as seen by his insistence on vertical integration, his concentration on building a reliable charging infrastructure, and his quest for breakthroughs in battery technology.

SpaceX work done by Musk is equally intriguing. Government organizations and well-established aerospace corporations, with their exorbitant costs and propensity for failure, had long controlled the space business. Musk promised to lower the cost of space travel so that people could colonize Mars, which seemed bold, if not impossible. However, SpaceX has reached goals that many believed would take decades to reach because to a combination of creative engineering, wise alliances, and an iterative development process. Falcon rockets' successful landing and subsequent reuse are evidence of a mindset that views setbacks as opportunities for growth and continuous improvement. Musk's visionary leadership at SpaceX emphasizes the importance of perseverance and a steadfast commitment to the goal, even in the face of major setbacks.

Satya Nadella's leadership of Microsoft has transformed the company, providing yet another compelling illustration of a successful business mindset. Many believed that Microsoft had passed its prime and was unable to adjust to a fast evolving business dominated by cloud services and mobile computing when Nadella assumed the role of CEO in 2014. Nadella's humble, empathetic, and growth-oriented approach played a key role in bringing the firm back to life. He brought about a culture change at Microsoft, emphasizing inclusivity, growth attitude, and teamwork instead of internal rivalry and rigidity.

Nadella has revolutionized the cloud computing industry with his strategic concentration on the platform, especially with the creation and growth of Azure. He led Microsoft away from its historical emphasis on Windows and Office software and toward a future where cloud solutions were essential after realizing the growing significance of cloud services. This change of direction not only created new sources of income for Microsoft but also established it as a leader in a field that is essential to the contemporary digital economy. When combined with a well-defined strategic vision, Nadella's ability to cultivate a culture of ongoing learning and adaptation highlights the significant influence of a growth-oriented corporate philosophy.

The tale of Howard Schultz and Starbucks serves as another evidence of how innovation and growth can be spurred by a strong business strategy. In the early 1980s, Starbucks was a little network of coffee shops in Seattle when Schultz started working there. Schultz imagined Starbucks as a "third place" between home and work, where people might congregate and drink premium coffee in a welcoming environment, influenced by the Italian coffee culture he encountered. His goal was to create an experience rather than just sell coffee.

Scaling this idea required a mindset that Schultz provided. As Starbucks quickly grew, he concentrated on upholding quality and consistency while placing a strong emphasis on staff development and customer support. At the time, it was a bold move for him to provide stock options and health benefits to part-time workers, which inspired loyalty and dedication in the workforce. Starbucks was able to expand from a local coffee business to a worldwide brand because to Schultz's ability to combine vision and operational competence.

But Starbucks was severely impacted by the 2008 financial crisis, which resulted in store closures and falling revenues. After taking over as CEO once more, Schultz oversaw a turnaround by emphasizing innovation and restating the company's basic principles. He made technological investments in the form of the Starbucks app and mobile ordering, and he also increased the range of products to include food and tea.

During this time, Schultz's leadership demonstrated the value of resilience, flexibility, and a dedication to fundamental values in overcoming obstacles in the commercial world.

Indra Nooyi's argument at PepsiCo is another strong one. Nooyi took on the dual challenge of addressing the company's expanding health and nutrition concerns and maintaining profitability when she was appointed CEO in 2006. PepsiCo's product line underwent a major change as a result of Nooyi's strategic thinking and emphasis on sustainability. Recognizing the long-term benefits of matching the company's offers with customer trends towards wellness, she championed the change towards healthier options.

The goal of PepsiCo, which is to generate sustainable growth by making investments in a better future for people and the world, was reinterpreted by Nooyi's emphasis on performance with purpose. This involved lowering the amount of sugar in drinks, lowering the amount of sodium and saturated fats in snacks, and diversifying the line to include healthier options. Her leadership serves as an example of how crucial it is to match corporate strategy with societal demands and shows how a visionary approach can lead to both profitability and beneficial influence.

Spanx and Sara Blakely's story is just another inspiring illustration of a successful business approach. Blakely changed the shapewear market when she started Spanx with barely $5,000 in savings. Her quest started with a straightforward yet impactful idea: to develop a more useful and comfortable substitute for conventional women's underwear. Blakely had little experience in the fashion or business worlds, but her attitude was determined, inventive, and centered around her product.

Early on, she encountered a great deal of resistance and setbacks, from shops doubting her idea's ability to find a market to manufacturers discounting it. But Blakely's capacity for perseverance and adaptation was essential. She negotiated a ground-breaking contract with Neiman Marcus, personally presented her goods to department stores, and used word-of-mouth advertising to increase brand awareness. The success of Spanx, which led to its growth into a billion-dollar business, highlights the value of having an optimistic outlook that welcomes obstacles and keeps one's eyes on the prize in spite of them.

The story of Alan Mulally's transformation of Ford Motor Company offers yet another powerful example of a successful business philosophy. Ford was experiencing financial difficulties, a lack of competitive products, and a diminishing market share when Mulally assumed the role of CEO in 2006. Mulally's strategy was based on open communication, collaboration, and an unwavering attention to the main objective.

He carried out the One Ford initiative, which prioritized budgetary restraint, operational effectiveness, and worldwide product development. Mulally dismantled organizational silos and promoted a climate of accountability and cooperation. His inclusive attitude and effective communication style aided in uniting the staff behind a common goal. Under his direction, Ford regained profitability, simplified its product selection, and effectively weathered the 2008 financial crisis without needing a government bailout. Mulally's tenure demonstrates how an inclusive, honest, and goal-oriented approach can propel a successful recovery under the most trying conditions.

Last but not least, the tale of Airbnb and its founders, Nathan Blecharczyk, Joe Gebbia, and Brian Chesky, sheds light on the significance of an inventive and tenacious mentality in overcoming initial obstacles. The founders of Airbnb came up with the idea to rent out air mattresses in their apartment for a conference because they needed the money for rent. There were many obstacles to overcome for this straightforward concept, such as doubts regarding the legitimacy and safety of short-term house rentals.

On the other hand, the founders' mentality was marked by inventiveness, tenacity, and a readiness to make adjustments in response to criticism. They expanded their offers and fixed consumer complaints to continuously improve their platform. Their flexibility, as demonstrated by their early fundraising efforts to sell unique cereal boxes, shows that they have an inventive and flexible mentality. Currently a worldwide phenomenon, Airbnb is upending the hospitality sector and serving as an example of how an inventive mentality can take a basic concept and turn it into a multibillion-dollar company.

Together, these case studies highlight the significant influence of an effective business mentality. A mindset that embraces challenges, learns from failures, and remains steadfast in the pursuit of long-term goals unites the visionary foresight of Reed Hastings at Netflix, the relentless innovation of Elon Musk at Tesla and SpaceX, the transformative leadership of Satya Nadella at Microsoft, and the resilience and creativity of Sara Blakely at Spanx. This kind of thinking is not just for founders and CEOs; it can be developed at all organizational levels and is crucial for negotiating the intricacies of the modern corporate world.

In conclusion, these executives' and their businesses' tales offer a compelling illustration of the significance of having a successful business attitude. They demonstrate how a mindset that prioritizes resilience, adaptability, vision, and ongoing learning may lead to success rather than just great ideas or advantageous market circumstances. Adopting such a mindset will be essential for people and organizations looking to succeed as we move forward in a world that is always changing.

CHAPTER 2

THE FOUNDATION OF LEADERSHIP

"Growing oneself is the key to success before
you become a leader. Being a leader means
that your main responsibility is to develop
others.
-"JACK WELCH"

"The requirement to have a vision is
fundamental to leadership. It must be a vision
you can express with conviction and clarity at
all times. You cannot sound a trumpet
indecisively.
-"Reverend Theodore M. Hesburgh

WHAT MAKES A LEADER?

Scholars, professionals, and the general public have all been captivated by the intricate and varied phenomenon of leadership for ages. It's common knowledge that "leaders are made, not born," implying that one can acquire the traits of successful leadership via training, experience, and deliberate effort. However, what really defines a leader? Numerous perspectives, including those from psychology, sociology, organizational behavior, and history, have been used to examine this issue. In order to comprehend the qualities of a leader, one must examine the traits, actions, and environments that allow people to motivate, sway, and direct others toward shared objectives.

Fundamentally, leadership is about having an impact. A leader may motivate and inspire others to realize a vision or objective. Not all influential leaders have formal authority; in fact, some of the most significant ones have very little of it. Rather, their power comes from a blend of character traits, actions, and interpersonal dynamics that foster confidence and inspire others to follow.

Emotional intelligence is one of a leader's most important qualities. Self-awareness, self-regulation, empathy, motivation, and social skills are all included in emotional intelligence. Emotionally intelligent leaders are skilled in both identifying and influencing other people's feelings as well as comprehending and controlling their own. Being able to emotionally connect with others promotes loyalty and trust, two qualities that are necessary for good leadership. For example, morale and cohesiveness are more likely to be maintained by a leader who can identify the dissatisfaction or fear that their team may be feeling during difficult times and respond to these feelings in a positive way.

A crucial aspect of emotional intelligence, empathy is especially significant in leadership roles. Leaders that possess empathy are able to comprehend the needs and viewpoints of others, which improves communication and decision-making. When leaders genuinely care about the welfare of their team members, a supportive environment is fostered where people feel appreciated and inspired to put out their best efforts. This is demonstrated by leaders such as New Zealand's Prime Minister Jacinda Ardern, who gained broad respect and trust for her compassionate handling of crises like the COVID-19 pandemic and the killings at the Christchurch mosque.

Another crucial component of leadership is vision. A leader's vision gives people and organizations purpose and direction, directing their actions toward a desired future. Proficient leaders possess the ability to not only express an enticing vision but also motivate others to accept and strive towards it. This calls for a combination of strategic thinking and the capacity to persuade others of the vision in a way that speaks to their beliefs and goals. The speech "I Have a Dream" by Martin Luther King Jr. is a classic illustration of visionary leadership. His ability to envision a time when racial justice and equality would be the norm ignited a movement and motivated millions of people to work for change.

But vision isn't enough; leaders also need to be able to carry out their vision. To accomplish the intended results, this entails establishing precise goals, creating strategies, and allocating resources. Strong organizational abilities, the capability to assign, and the flexibility to adjust to changing conditions are necessary for effective execution. To ensure that the vision is turned into workable strategies and quantifiable achievements, leaders must strike a balance between the big picture and the details.

Being flexible is an essential quality for leaders, especially in the fast-paced, unpredictable world of today. Maintaining success requires the ability to adapt to change, whether it comes from global events, market adjustments, or technology improvements. Adaptive leaders are receptive to fresh perspectives, risk-takers, and capable of picking up lessons from mistakes. Within their companies, they promote an innovative and constant improvement culture. The quick ascent and prosperity of businesses such as Amazon and Google can be partly ascribed to the flexible leadership of individuals such as Jeff Bezos and Sundar Pichai, who have consistently guided their organizations through changing environments.

Resilience is a crucial attribute of proficient leaders, closely linked to adaptability. Leaders that possess resilience are able to bear setbacks and bounce back, staying focused and unwavering in the face of difficulty. This trait, which creates leaders who are not readily deterred by setbacks, is frequently developed via both personal and professional struggles. Teams under the leadership of resilient individuals are more confident because they see that obstacles can be surmounted with tenacity and a positive outlook. Throughout her tenure, Angela Merkel, the former German Chancellor, demonstrated remarkable resilience by leading her nation with poise and composure through periods of economic turmoil, refugee inflows, and political upheavals.

For leaders, effective communication is essential because it's the foundation of their capacity to motivate and inspire others. Transmitting information is only one aspect of effective communication; other tasks include attentively listening, comprehending the target audience, and articulating ideas in an engaging way. Effective communicators are able to express their vision, offer helpful criticism, and encourage candid discussion among their team members. This fosters an atmosphere in which concepts may be discussed openly and problems can be resolved together. Barack Obama is a prime example of the value of excellent communication in leadership due to his eloquence and capacity to engage a wide range of audiences in his speeches and public appearances.

Another essential component of leadership is integrity. Honest, moral, and consistent in their deeds and choices are characteristics of leaders with integrity. By keeping themselves to high standards of behavior and by coordinating their words and deeds, they establish confidence. Integrity helps companies develop a transparent and moral culture that promotes sustainability and long-term success. Nelson Mandela is a prime example of the significant influence of integrity in leadership due to his continuous dedication to justice and equality, even at tremendous personal cost.

Effective leadership is influenced not only by these personal attributes but also by the capacity to establish and maintain relationships. Building solid, cooperative connections with colleagues, stakeholders, and team members is crucial for leaders. This entails establishing a feeling of community, encouraging teamwork, and comprehending the motivations and strengths of others. In order to achieve group objectives, relational leadership places a strong emphasis on inclusivity, diversity, and respect for one another. Leaders using a relational approach—such as Indra Nooyi, the former CEO of PepsiCo—are well-known for stressing the value of taking care of staff members and fostering a positive work atmosphere.

Being a leader also means having to make tough choices and accept accountability for the results. Making decisions is a complicated process that calls for carefully weighing the interests of many stakeholders, prospective outcomes, and the information that is currently accessible. Proficient leaders has the ability to promptly make decisions despite ambiguity and maintain their integrity. They use their experience and insights to inform their decisions, striking a balance between logical thinking and intuition. Decision-making in times of crisis is crucial, as demonstrated by Winston Churchill's leadership during World War II, which was marked by his firm and decisive decisions.

Moreover, the key to a leader's efficacy lies in their capacity to encourage and inspire others. Leaders that inspire others possess a contagious passion and energy that excite and motivate others. They provide an exemplary example for others to follow by working diligently and well. Establishing elevated benchmarks and motivating individuals to realize their complete potential fosters a climate of superiority and ongoing enhancement. Leaders such as Steve Jobs inspired his staff to accomplish remarkable achievements at Apple with his unwavering enthusiasm for invention and perfection.

The environment in which leadership takes place also has a big impact on how effective it is. Different leadership philosophies and techniques are needed for various circumstances. For example, transformational leadership works best in circumstances that are dynamic and changing quickly since it entails inspiring and empowering others to achieve higher levels of performance. In contrast, predictable, routine circumstances may be more suited for transactional leadership, which emphasizes rewards, clear structures, and performance monitoring. Proficient leaders exhibit situational awareness and adaptability by evaluating the requirements of their surroundings and modifying their approach accordingly.

Furthermore, leadership is not limited to official positions of power. Informal leaders are just as essential; even though they don't have titles, they nevertheless have a big impact on their groups or communities. These people frequently provide an example for others to follow by their deeds and behaviors, and they motivate others with their dedication and honesty. The concept of informal leadership emphasizes that becoming a leader is a team effort requiring the efforts of numerous people at various levels.

Gaining leadership abilities and traits is a lifetime process. While some people may be born leaders, the most successful ones are those that constantly hone their craft by education, experience, and introspection. The development of leadership potential is facilitated by real-world problems, mentorship, and leadership development programs. Businesses that invest in their leaders' development build a talent pool of people who are more equipped to meet obstacles in the future and achieve success.

Furthermore, leadership has an impact that transcends corporate boundaries. Leaders have the power to affect more general societal and international challenges. For example, social and political leaders are essential in determining public policy, correcting injustices, and promoting social progress. Their capacity to unite individuals and assets in support of shared objectives has the potential to profoundly alter society. Leadership exemplified by individuals such as Mahatma Gandhi, who spearheaded India's nonviolent independence movement, demonstrates the significant influence that visionary and ethical leadership can have on society.

Leaders face more difficult issues than ever in the linked and fast changing world of today. Technological innovations, globalization, and socio-political shifts have created a world in which ethics, creativity, and adaptability are critical. A mindset that welcomes change, encourages teamwork, and places a high value on sustainability and social responsibility is necessary for leaders to successfully negotiate these challenges.

Tim Cook of Apple is one modern example of this kind of leadership. Cook faced the enormous challenge of succeeding Steve Jobs as CEO, having followed in the footsteps of a great leader. Apple's success has been sustained in large part due to Cook's leadership style, which is defined by an emphasis on operational excellence, inclusion, and social responsibility. His support of programs pertaining to diversity and inclusion, privacy, and environmental sustainability is indicative of a more comprehensive view of leadership that goes beyond financial gain to consider the impact on society.

In a similar vein, the late Marriott International CEO Arne Sorenson's leadership emphasizes the value of compassion and social responsibility. Sorenson placed a strong emphasis on corporate responsibility, diversity and inclusion, and employee well-being in his leadership style. Sorenson demonstrated transparency in its communication with employees and implemented noteworthy measures to provide support during the COVID-19 epidemic, despite the hospitality sector encountering unparalleled difficulties. His leadership served as an example of how moral accountability and compassion are essential to maintaining an organization's performance and resilience.

It becomes clear when we think about what constitutes a leader that effective leadership is not characterized by a single set of traits or actions. Rather, it is the result of a dynamic interaction between ambient elements, relational dynamics, and personal traits. Leaders use their vision, emotional intelligence, flexibility, and integrity to motivate and sway others. They make wise decisions, establish trusting bonds with others, and communicate clearly. They are dedicated to lifelong learning and development and strong in the face of adversity.

In the end, a leader is someone who can mentor others toward a common goal, creating a feeling of direction and teamwork. Whether in an organization, a community, or society at large, the goal of leadership is to bring about constructive change. It's about enabling people to reach their full potential and making a positive impact on the future. The need for visionary, moral, and capable leadership is greater than ever as the globe changes. We can better manage the complexity of our time and create a more inclusive, sustainable, and successful world if we comprehend and nurture the traits of a leader.

KEY LEADERSHIP QUALITIES

A great deal of research and reflection has been done on leadership, which is a crucial component of human connection and organizational performance. Even though the situations and difficulties may change, the fundamental characteristics of a successful leader are strikingly constant. Great leadership is based on these characteristics, which affect how leaders encourage, inspire, and direct their followers toward accomplishing shared objectives. It is crucial for people in leadership roles as well as anyone hoping to have a significant impact on both their personal and professional lives to comprehend these fundamental leadership traits.

Effective leadership is fundamentally based on emotional intelligence. The ability to identify, comprehend, and regulate one's own emotions as well as those of others is referred to as emotional intelligence. Empathic, self-aware, and capable of controlling their emotions are traits of leaders with high emotional intelligence. Leaders that are self-aware are able to see their own advantages and disadvantages, which is essential for both personal development and productive leadership. Leaders may create a more happy and productive workplace by better managing their reactions and interactions with others by being aware of their emotional triggers and responses.

Leaders can establish stronger connections with their team members by demonstrating empathy, which is a crucial aspect of emotional intelligence. Empathetic leaders are able to relate to and comprehend the emotions of others, building rapport and trust. In order to address team members' needs and problems and increase engagement and loyalty, this understanding is crucial. Employee motivation and commitment to their work are more likely when they feel respected and heard. Additionally, a leader with empathy is better able to handle interpersonal problems and create solutions that take into account the viewpoints and welfare of all parties.

Vision is another essential component of successful leadership. Leaders with vision are able to inspire and motivate people by communicating their goals in an understandable and captivating manner. The decisions and actions of a leader and their followers are guided by a compelling vision that gives them direction and purpose. It serves as a beacon, guiding the company through difficulties and keeping it concentrated on long-term objectives. Not only can visionary leaders see the big picture, but they can also turn their ideas into workable plans and tactics. They can ensure that progress is made towards the final objective by breaking down the vision into attainable milestones.

But vision alone is insufficient for leaders; they also need to be skilled at conveying it. Effective communication is a vital component of leadership because it allows leaders to communicate their thoughts, expectations, and criticism in a clear and compelling way. Active listening, clarity, and the capacity to modify messages for various audiences are all necessary for effective communication. Effective communicators are able to inspire their team to take action by clearly expressing their vision and goals. They also offer team members helpful criticism that enables them to see their areas of strength and growth. A culture of trust and cooperation is fostered by open and honest communication, which makes team members feel comfortable discussing their thoughts and worries.

Yet another essential component of successful leadership is adaptability. Leaders today need to be able to navigate ambiguity and adjust to changing conditions in a world that is changing quickly. This necessitates being open to change, able to draw lessons from past mistakes, and adaptable when faced with difficulties. Adaptive leaders are receptive to fresh perspectives and methods and are always looking for ways to innovate and get better. They know that failure is frequently an essential step on the path to success, so they don't hesitate to take chances and adjust course when needed. Leaders may help their firms remain resilient and competitive in the face of change by promoting an adaptable culture.

As flexibility and resilience go hand in hand, the former is necessary to maintain leadership effectiveness over the long haul. Despite obstacles, resilient leaders are able to overcome setbacks and keep their resolve and concentration. Rather than seeing difficulties as insurmountable barriers, they see them as chances for development and education. They are able to endure adversity and motivate their colleagues to do the same because of their optimistic outlook. Experience, as well as the capacity to control stress and preserve equilibrium, are key factors in the development of resilience. Leaders who put their health first and take care of themselves are better able to cope with the responsibilities and stress of their roles.

The fundamental characteristic of integrity serves as the basis for all other facets of successful leadership. Honest, moral, and consistent in their deeds and choices are characteristics of leaders with integrity. They gain followers' trust and credibility by being consistent in both their words and acts. Maintaining integrity entails upholding a strict moral code and making morally sound decisions, especially when doing so is challenging or unpopular. Integrity-driven leaders foster an environment of accountability and openness where team members have faith in the goals and deeds of their leader. Building loyalty and dedication, resolving moral conundrums, and upholding the good name of the company all depend on this trust.

The capacity to uplift and motivate people is a crucial component of good leadership. Passionate and energizing, inspirational leaders inspire their followers to be enthusiastic and committed. They provide an exemplary example for others to follow by working diligently and well. Empowering others to realize their full potential and establishing high expectations for excellence, inspirational leaders foster a culture of constant growth. They encourage a sense of satisfaction and accomplishment in their team members by acknowledging and celebrating their accomplishments. This kind of feedback keeps people motivated and encourages further effort.

Another essential component of good leadership is the ability to establish and maintain relationships. Relationships with teammates, peers, and stakeholders are an integral part of being a leader. Within an organization, leaders can foster a feeling of community and belonging by developing strong, cooperative relationships. This entails establishing an open atmosphere, encouraging teamwork, and being aware of the motivations and strengths of others. Relational leaders give their team members' growth and well-being first priority and offer guidance and support. To accomplish common objectives, leaders can use the combined abilities and endeavors of their team by fostering an environment of mutual esteem and cooperation.

Making decisions is a critical component of leadership since it is frequently necessary for leaders to make difficult and important choices. Making decisions that are ethically sound requires combining intuition, critical reasoning, and intuitive feeling. It is imperative for leaders to collect and assess pertinent data, contemplate possible outcomes, and balance the concerns of many stakeholders. They must also possess the ability to decide quickly, even in the face of ambiguity and uncertainty. This calls for self-assurance and the capacity to accept accountability for the results of their choices. Good leaders seek out the opinions and input of people while involving their team in decision-making. This team-based methodology not only improves decision quality but also cultivates a feeling of commitment and responsibility among team members.

People like Elon Musk, whose ability to predict and capitalize on emerging trends has transformed everything from electric vehicles to space exploration, are prime examples of visionary leadership. Not only did Musk want to build electric vehicles, but he also wanted to shift the entire automotive sector to use more sustainable forms of energy. This goal included developing solar products, improving battery technology, and constructing a complete charging infrastructure. His audacious objectives, like using SpaceX to bring human life to multiple planets, highlight the need of having a visionary mentality. Musk's vision is relentlessly pursued, motivating his teams to accomplish what many thought was impossible. This is a hallmark of his leadership style. His accomplishments serve as a reminder of how crucial visionary leadership is to fostering creativity and long-term success.

The leadership of Facebook's Chief Operating Officer, Sheryl Sandberg, is a striking example of effective communication. Facebook has grown and faced crises, but Sandberg's ability to communicate the company's vision and ideals has been essential to the company's success. Building trust with external stakeholders and within the company has been facilitated by her emphasis on transparency and open communication style. Sandberg's emphasis on open, honest communication is especially noticeable in her initiatives to combat gender inequity, such as her support of women in leadership roles and her book "Lean In." She has encouraged many others to have thoughtful conversations on workplace diversity and inclusion by sharing her personal experiences and ideas. Through his leadership, Sandberg shows how good communication can create trust, strengthen bonds between people, and propel an organization to success.

The attributes that characterize Microsoft CEO Satya Nadella's leadership include adaptability and resilience. When Nadella became CEO in 2014, many thought of Microsoft as a tech behemoth that was stagnant and had trouble moving with the times. Nadella's ability to adapt to change and take decisive action to reposition

Microsoft for the future was a defining characteristic of his leadership. He turned the company's attention to artificial intelligence and cloud computing, making Microsoft a leader in both fields. Microsoft's comeback has been largely attributed to Nadella's adaptability to new technological developments and his fortitude in the face of difficulties. His leadership serves as a reminder of how crucial it is to be resilient and adaptive when negotiating complicated and changing corporate environments.

Effective leadership is built on integrity, as Berkshire Hathaway CEO Warren Buffett has shown. Buffett has gained the respect and admiration of investors, staff members, and the general public due to his reputation for integrity, honesty, and openness. He is renowned for his honest communication approach, humility while accepting criticism, and dedication to moral corporate conduct. At Berkshire Hathaway, a strong corporate culture where employees are encouraged to operate with honesty and accountability has been built in large part thanks to Buffett's ethics. His leadership serves as an example of how honesty builds credibility and trust, all of which are necessary for long-term success and fostering good relationships with stakeholders.

The leadership exemplified by the youngest Nobel laureate, Malala Yousafzai, is one of inspiration and drive. Millions of people all throughout the world have been inspired by Malala's support of girls' education and her brave resistance to the Taliban. She has persisted in her goal despite being in potentially fatal danger and has used her platform to elevate the voices of underrepresented girls. Malala's ability to inspire action and change, her capacity to connect with people via her experience, and her steadfast dedication to her cause are what define her leadership. Her leadership demonstrates the powerful effect that inspiration and motivation can have on bringing people together in support of a common objective.

The ability to establish and maintain relationships is demonstrated by former Starbucks CEO Howard Schultz. Under Schultz's direction, Starbucks aimed to foster a feeling of connection and community among its staff and patrons. He underlined how crucial it is to treat staff members with dignity and give them chances for advancement. With the goal of turning Starbucks into a "third place" where people might feel at ease and connected, Schultz's relational approach also extended to his patrons. His leadership serves as an example of how fostering strong bonds between people may improve company culture and increase consumer loyalty.

As the previous German Chancellor Angela Merkel has shown, decision-making abilities are essential for successful leadership. Merkel demonstrated cautious and thoughtful decision-making throughout her leadership during a number of crises, such as the European debt crisis and the refugee crisis. She conducted in-depth research, spoke with specialists, and thought carefully about the long-term effects of her choices. Merkel's self-assurance and dedication to moral values were shown by her capacity to make difficult choices despite resistance.

Her example of leadership demonstrates how crucial it is to make morally sound judgments and accept accountability for the results.

In summary, a blend of essential attributes that allow leaders to motivate, sway, and mentor people toward shared objectives define effective leadership. Effective leadership requires a variety of qualities, including emotional intelligence, vision, communication skills, adaptability, resilience, integrity, the capacity to build relationships, the ability to inspire and encourage others, and decision-making abilities. These are not intrinsic qualities; rather, they can be cultivated and improved by education, experience, and introspection. People can become more effective leaders and have a significant impact on both their personal and professional life by comprehending and developing these attributes. The need for visionary, moral, and capable leadership is greater than ever as the globe changes. Leaders may successfully negotiate the challenges of our day and create a more affluent, sustainable, and inclusive future by adopting five essential traits.

LEADERSHIP VS MANAGEMENT

Although they represent different ideas and functions, the terms leadership and management are frequently used synonymously in the field of organisational dynamics. Anyone hoping to succeed in the workplace has to understand the subtle differences between management and leadership, since both are essential to the success of an organisation. Although there is a lot of overlap between the two, they differ in terms of their primary purposes, areas of emphasis, and effects on individuals and procedures. By examining these distinctions, we can see how management and leadership both specifically contribute to the accomplishment of corporate objectives and the reasons that both are necessary for a productive, harmonious workplace.

At its most basic, management is the process of allocating, allocating, and coordinating resources in order to accomplish particular goals. Managers are in charge of upholding consistency, streamlining procedures, and making sure that things go well on a daily basis. Their primary concerns are productivity, efficiency, and following set protocols and guidelines. A manager's job is by its very nature administrative; it involves things like scheduling, budgeting, and performance evaluation. In order to achieve organisational objectives, managers define goals, assign resources, and supervise the application of strategies. They give workers the resources and direction they need to carry out their jobs well in addition to making sure they are aware of their roles and obligations.

On the other side, leadership entails motivating and persuading others to realise a common goal. Motivating and empowering people, encouraging creativity, and accelerating change are the main objectives of leaders. Leaders are focused on the growth of people, whereas managers are more concerned with procedures and frameworks. Establishing a vision, bringing others into alignment with it, and motivating them to act are all parts of leadership. By fostering a feeling of direction and purpose in their followers, leaders inspire them to go above their daily responsibilities and make a positive impact on society. They foster an atmosphere that encourages people to realise their full potential and values initiative and innovation.

The way management and leadership handle change is one of their main differences. In order to preserve consistency and reduce risks, managers frequently work inside pre-existing frameworks. Usually, they are focused on making the organisation function well and streamlining current processes. Achieving short-term objectives and preserving operational effectiveness depend on this emphasis on stability and order. Managers are adept at looking at data, pinpointing areas that need work, and putting solutions in place to boost output. To make sure the company reaches its goals and stays within its budget, they base their decisions on well-established measurements and benchmarks.

On the other hand, leaders frequently act as change agents. They challenge the status quo and encourage others to embrace change by seeing new possibilities and chances. Leaders are progressive; they are always looking for new and creative ways to do things better. They are prepared to take chances in order to succeed over the long run because they understand that change is essential for progress. Leaders encourage those they follow to take on fresh viewpoints, acquire new abilities, and set new objectives. They foster an environment of ongoing development where learning and experimentation are valued. Leaders set their organisations up for success by encouraging a resilient and adaptive mentality that helps them deal with the complexities and uncertainties of the future.

The way that management and leadership emphasise people differently from tasks further illustrates this relationship. In order to ensure that work is done properly and efficiently, managers typically prioritise jobs and procedures. To make sure that workers fulfil performance criteria, they are worried about establishing clear expectations, keeping an eye on development, and offering feedback. To make sure that everyone abides by company regulations, managers utilise their power to enforce rules and processes. They are frequently viewed as problem solvers, taking care of problems as they come up and coming up with fixes to keep things running smoothly.

On the other hand, leaders put people first. They put money into fostering relationships, getting to know their followers' wants and goals, and fostering an atmosphere where people are encouraged and felt appreciated. Since people are an organization's most valuable resource, leaders concentrate on helping them reach their full potential. They serve as coaches and mentors, offering direction and support to aid in people's development on both a personal and professional level. By granting individuals the freedom to decide for themselves and accept responsibility for their job, leaders enable their followers. Employee loyalty and dedication are increased as a result of this people-focused approach since they feel a connection to both the organization's goal and their leader.

Their divergent approaches to motivating constitute a fundamental component of the leadership versus management conflict. Extrinsic motivators, like prizes and incentives, are frequently used by managers to boost output. They create objectives, give precise directions, and present observable advantages to encourage staff members to meet targets. This strategy might work well for short-term goals, but it might not be able to maintain long-term engagement and satisfaction. To sustain high levels of motivation and performance, managers must strike a balance between using extrinsic motivators and other tactics.

On the other hand, leaders mostly depend on internal motivators. By assisting them in finding meaning in their job and relating it to a greater cause, they motivate and inspire those who follow them. Leaders know that people are driven by a feeling of achievement, the chance to improve personally, and the chance to make a meaningful contribution. Leaders create an environment where people are inspired to perform well and come up with new ideas by cultivating a culture of appreciation and acknowledgement. Because people are motivated by a strong feeling of fulfilment and purpose, intrinsic motivation fosters long-term engagement and commitment.

Processes used to make decisions can draw attention to the distinctions between management and leadership. Typically, managers use predefined frameworks and norms to inform their decisions, which are based on data and analysis. When weighing options and deciding on the best course of action, they rely on quantitative measures and performance indicators. This methodical process guarantees that choices are supported by data and in line with the objectives of the company. In order to make sure that decisions are well-informed and practical, managers often include their team members in the decision-making process by asking for comments and suggestions.

On the other hand, leaders frequently use vision and intuition to inform their choices. Even when all the knowledge is not available to them, they are not afraid to take chances and make audacious decisions. Leaders negotiate difficult and unclear situations by following their gut feelings and drawing from past experiences. They may make decisions that don't necessarily follow common wisdom since they are at ease with uncertainty. Through the adoption of a visionary mindset, leaders can stimulate creativity and generate fresh prospects for expansion and achievement. They are able to make strategic decisions that position their organisation for long-term success because of their ability to see the big picture and predict future trends.

The ways that management and leadership handle dispute further highlight the differences between the two roles. When resolving disputes, managers typically follow formalised protocols with the goal of identifying workable solutions that comply with company guidelines. They ensure that problems are settled quickly and effectively by using their power to mediate disputes. Since unresolved disputes can impair performance and productivity, managers prioritise preserving peace and causing the fewest possible disturbances.

On the other hand, leaders approach dispute resolution with an emphasis on empathy and understanding. They understand that fundamental problems and divergent viewpoints frequently give birth to confrontations. Leaders pay attention to what everyone has to say, trying to grasp their worries and points of view. Leaders may address the underlying causes of conflicts and create solutions that meet the requirements of all parties by encouraging open communication and providing a safe environment for discussion. In addition to resolving disputes, this compassionate method fortifies bonds and fosters team trust.

Organisational success depends on both management and leadership, and the best managers and leaders frequently possess both skills. Despite having distinct skill sets and objectives, management and leadership are complimentary and interdependent. Managers are essential to an organization's ability to maintain daily operations, optimise resource use, and meet performance goals. Managers provide an organisation the consistency and stability it needs to run well, which helps it accomplish its short-term objectives.

Organisations require leaders who can foster innovation, encourage staff members, and manage change. Leaders inspire others to think creatively and seize new chances by providing the vision and guidance necessary for long-term success. They foster an environment of empowerment and engagement where workers are inspired to put forth their best work. Organisations can build a dynamic and resilient environment that supports growth and stability by striking a balance between the capabilities of management and leadership.

The technology sector provides a clear illustration of how management and leadership interact. Leaders like Sundar Pichai and Tim Cook at businesses like Google and Apple have proven to be adept at striking a balance between visionary leadership and efficient management. Pichai's emphasis on innovation and user-centric design is a defining feature of his leadership at Google, motivating his teams to create ground-breaking goods and services. Simultaneously, he exhibits outstanding managerial qualities by guaranteeing that Google's operations are effective and in line with strategic objectives. Cook, on the other side, has optimised Apple's supply chain and operational procedures while upholding the company's reputation for excellence and innovation. Maintaining Apple's success in a very competitive industry has been made possible by his ability to strike a balance between management and leadership.

The differences between management and leadership are also noticeable in the healthcare industry. Healthcare managers are in charge of making sure that patient care requirements are fulfilled, resources are distributed wisely, and hospitals and clinics run smoothly. Their main priorities are process optimisation, budget management, and regulatory compliance. On the other hand, leaders in the healthcare industry encourage and inspire their staff to deliver patient-centered, compassionate care. They lead programmes that improve patient outcomes, cultivate a culture of continuous improvement, and establish a vision for excellence in healthcare delivery. Healthcare organisations can attain both operational efficiency and high-quality patient care by striking a balance between leadership and management.

Another industry where management and leadership must work together is education. Budgeting, staffing, and curriculum planning are just a few of the administrative tasks that fall under the purview of school principals and district managers. They guarantee that schools run efficiently and fulfil academic requirements. On the other hand, motivating educators, learners, and parents to pursue greatness is another essential function of educational leaders. They develop an optimistic and welcoming school climate, spearhead programmes that improve student performance, and provide a vision for academic achievement. Skilled educators strike a balance between their administrative responsibilities and their capacity to uplift and encourage their communities.

In conclusion, even though they are two different ideas, management and leadership are both crucial to the development of an organisation. The basic goals of management are to preserve stability, streamline procedures, and guarantee effective operations. To accomplish particular goals, managers assign tasks, set targets, and track performance. On the other side, leadership entails motivating and persuading others to realise a common goal. Leaders encourage creativity, empower others, and bring about change. They foster an atmosphere that encourages people to realise their full potential and values initiative and innovation.

Management and leadership have a complicated and intertwined relationship. Strong managerial abilities are frequently exhibited by effective leaders, and effective managers also show leadership traits. To succeed in the long run and operate efficiently in the short term, organisations require both management and leadership. Through comprehending the distinctions and synergies between management and leadership, people can acquire the competencies required to flourish in their positions and leave a lasting impression on their companies. The capacity to strike a balance between management and leadership will become more and more important as the world changes in order to successfully navigate its complexity and uncertainty.

SELF ASSESSMENT: ARE YOU A LEADER?

Self-reflection and evaluation are the first steps on the path to discovering whether or not one has leadership potential. The enquiry, "Are you a leader?" prompts an examination of an individual's characteristics, actions, and past encounters to ascertain the degree to which leadership is ingrained in their personality and capabilities. In the context of leadership, self-evaluation entails not just identifying one's areas of strength but also growth and development. It is a thorough assessment that takes into account many facets of a person's behaviour, values, and personality.

One must first examine their capacity to inspire and influence others before embarking on this road. At its core, leadership is about directing others towards a common vision or objective. Taking stock of previous instances in which you led a group effort, inspired colleagues, or started an initiative might help you identify your leadership potential. Not only may leadership be found in official responsibilities, but it can also be seen in everyday activities and unofficial roles. Maybe you've been the one others go to when they need help, or you've always taken the initiative in social situations. These experiences may suggest a natural aptitude for leadership.

Emotional intelligence assessment is a critical component of self-evaluation. Effective leadership is greatly influenced by emotional intelligence, which is comprised of social skills, self-awareness, self-regulation, and empathy. The cornerstone of emotional intelligence is self-awareness. It entails being aware of your feelings, your advantages and disadvantages, and how you affect other people. Getting input from others and thinking back on your feelings on a regular basis can help you become more self-aware. It's also critical to have emotional self-control, particularly under pressure. Leaders who remain composed and make deliberate choices when faced with challenges are more likely to gain the respect and confidence of their followers.

Another essential component of emotional intelligence and leadership is empathy, or the capacity to comprehend and experience another person's emotions. A leader who possesses empathy can establish a more profound connection with their team, fostering a welcoming and cooperative atmosphere. Think about how frequently you validate the sentiments of people, actively listen to them, and provide assistance. These actions promote loyalty and trust, two qualities that are crucial to good leadership. Strong social skills also help leaders resolve disagreements, promote cooperation, and establish and maintain beneficial connections. Think back on your connections and how well you are able to establish rapport and maintain them.

Strategic thought and vision are also essential components of leadership. A leader needs to be able to formulate plans to carry out their well-defined goals and accomplish those goals. Consider your ability to plan ahead and think ahead. Can you make plans that will help you reach long-term objectives? Are you able to foresee obstacles and modify your tactics accordingly? Painting a vivid picture of the future and uniting their team behind it are two ways that visionary leaders inspire others. Evaluating your strategic thinking skills and capacity to motivate others through your vision can tell you a lot about your leadership potential.

Effective communication is yet another essential facet of leadership. Proficient leaders listen intently, speak with clarity and conviction, and encourage candid conversation. Consider your interpersonal communication style. Can you properly communicate your ideas and thoughts? Do you actively listen to others and take into account their viewpoints? Can you provide and accept constructive criticism? Effective communication abilities empower leaders to express their ideas clearly, establish agreement, and cultivate an environment of openness and confidence.

Resilience and adaptability are crucial traits for leaders, particularly in the ever evolving world of today. Sustained leadership success requires the capacity to adjust to changing circumstances, welcome change, and overcome obstacles. Think back on your encounters with hardship and change. How do you handle unforeseen difficulties? Can you modify your plans and tactics to take into account fresh knowledge or evolving conditions? Resilient leaders encourage their team members to persist despite adversity by keeping a positive attitude.

Honesty and moral conduct are essential components of reliable leadership. Leaders need to exhibit integrity, equity, and a dedication to moral values on a regular basis. Think about your principles and how you apply them to your behaviour. Do you always behave honourably, even when it's challenging? Do you make choices based on moral principles and other people's best interests? Integrity in a leader fosters confidence and trust, all of which are necessary for successful leadership.

Another quality that sets a leader apart is their willingness to accept accountability. Being a leader is taking responsibility for both the team's and one's own decisions and actions. Think back on your encounters with accountability. Are you prepared to own up to your errors and grow from them? Do you hold people, including yourself, responsible for keeping your word and accomplishing your objectives? Responsible leaders promote an environment of accountability and ongoing development.

Finally, the formation of leadership requires a dedication to ongoing learning and progress. Consider your perspective on education and personal development. Are you receptive to fresh insights and experiences? Do you actively look for chances to advance your knowledge and abilities? Leaders who are dedicated to their own development also provide a better example for others and are better able to handle the challenges that come with being in a position of leadership.

Self-evaluation is a continuous process that calls for introspection, candour, and a readiness to accept change. It entails asking for input from others, thinking back on your encounters, and remaining receptive to both professional and personal growth. You can better understand your leadership potential by looking at your capacity for inspiring and influencing others, emotional intelligence, vision and strategic thinking, communication skills, adaptability and resilience, integrity, willingness to take on responsibility, and dedication to lifelong learning.

The route to being a successful leader is one of ongoing growth and development rather than a final goal. Whether you are in a formal leadership role now or would like to be in the future, self-evaluation is an important tool for developing your leadership skills. Accepting this path of self-improvement and learning will help you acquire the traits of a successful leader and have a significant impact on both your personal and professional lives. Being a leader is about being real, devoted, and open to learning, not about being flawless. You may unleash your leadership potential and start on a road of ongoing development and contribution by evaluating yourself.

CHAPTER 3

DEVELOPING LEADERSHIP SKILLS

"Concentrating on leadership development is the single most effective strategy to change a company. An organization with good people at its core, grooming them for leadership roles, and providing them with ongoing development opportunities has virtually endless potential.
-" John C. Maxwell"

EMOTIONAL INTELLIGENCE IN LEADERSHIP

Within the dynamic context of contemporary companies, the notion of leadership has beyond conventional limitations. Effective leadership now includes a greater grasp of human dynamics and interpersonal connections and is no longer limited to hierarchical structures or managerial functions alone. The idea of emotional intelligence (EI), a crucial element of effective leadership, lies at the center of this paradigm shift. The term "emotional intelligence" describes the capacity to identify, comprehend, control, and affect feelings in oneself and others. It stands for a critical nexus of cognitive and affective skills that enable leaders to engage with their teams, motivate them, and cultivate a climate of trust and cooperation.

The foundation of emotional intelligence in leadership is self-awareness. High self-awareness leaders are keenly aware of their feelings, motives, ideals, and strengths and shortcomings. Leaders who possess this enhanced self-awareness are more equipped to control their emotions, which helps them avoid rash decisions and guarantee considered answers. Leaders can control their behavior in a way that is consistent with their beliefs and objectives when they are aware of their emotional triggers and reactions. For example, when faced with a difficult project, a self-aware leader will identify their displeasure and respond positively instead of snapping at their staff. Team members feel appreciated and understood in a secure, encouraging work atmosphere that is fostered by this self-regulation.

Furthermore, self-awareness enables leaders to recognize how they affect other people. Leaders can modify their conduct to foster a pleasant and inspiring environment if they are aware of how their feelings and actions affect their team. This knowledge is essential for establishing credibility and trust since team members are more likely to follow a leader who exhibits empathy and consistency. To promote an environment of openness and support among team members, a leader who realizes that their own stress is negatively impacting their team's morale can take action to manage their own stress and engage in open communication with them.

Emotional intelligence in leadership goes beyond self-awareness and includes effective self-regulation—that is, the capacity to control one's impulses and feelings. Proficient in self-control enable leaders to remain composed and make logical choices, even under demanding circumstances. This skill is essential for fostering an atmosphere of consistency and predictability where team members can count on their leader to maintain composure and concentration. Self-regulatory leaders are less inclined to act rashly or emotionally, which helps avoid miscommunication and disputes within the team.

Moreover, self-regulation includes the ability to adapt, which is a necessary quality in the quickly evolving world of today. Leaders that possess the ability to modify their tactics and methods in reaction to fresh insights or changing situations are more proficient in steering their groups through ambiguity. For example, a leader may need to change course in response to an unforeseen shift in the market. Even in the face of difficulty, a leader who maintains composure and flexibility may make wise choices and give their team confidence.

Another essential element of emotional intelligence is empathy, which is crucial to leadership. Leaders who possess empathy are able to relate to their team members on a deeper level because they are able to comprehend and experience their emotions. Strong relationships and the development of a sense of commitment and belonging depend on this connection. When leaders display empathy, they are valuing their team members as people, not simply as workers. Team morale and motivation can be greatly increased by receiving this confirmation and acknowledgment.

Additionally, empathy enables leaders to successfully attend to the wants and concerns of their team members. Leaders are able to recognize any problems and take action before they become more serious by actively listening to and comprehending the opinions of their team. Team members feel heard and respected in this proactive approach to problem-solving, which creates a good and encouraging work atmosphere. When a team member is experiencing a lot of work, for instance, an understanding leader can provide resources and support to lighten the load, minimizing burnout and preserving productivity.

Social skills are just as important as empathy when it comes to emotional intelligence in leadership. A variety of talents are included under social skills, such as efficient communication, dispute resolution, and relationship building and maintenance. Strong social skills enable leaders to establish a cooperative and cohesive team environment while navigating challenging social dynamics. An essential component of these social skills is effective communication. Effective leaders are able to motivate their team and inspire collective action by communicating their vision, goals, and expectations in a clear and compelling manner. Moreover, leaders that actively listen to their team members and offer helpful criticism can raise productivity and engagement.

Resolving conflicts is yet another essential social ability for leaders. Conflicts are a given in any team. Leaders with high emotional intelligence, however, are able to resolve disputes amicably and to the satisfaction of all parties. Leaders may turn potential sources of dispute into chances for development and cooperation by approaching conflicts with empathy and an open mind. A leader who, for example, mediates a conflict between team members by encouraging a civil and honest discussion can assist in finding a solution while enhancing the group's cohesiveness and trust.

Another important aspect of social skills in leadership is establishing and sustaining relationships. Building a network of trust and support with colleagues, stakeholders, and team members is a key component of a leader's success in accomplishing corporate objectives. Leaders may harness varied viewpoints and talents to drive innovation and collective achievement by cultivating positive relationships. Furthermore, because they can depend on their network for assistance and cooperation, leaders with strong relationships are better equipped to deal with obstacles and disappointments.

Emotional intelligence has an impact on leadership that goes beyond interpersonal relationships to affect performance and organizational culture. A culture of trust, respect, and cooperation can be developed by leaders who place a high priority on emotional intelligence. This culture promotes employee engagement and satisfaction. Team members are more likely to be driven and devoted to their task when they feel appreciated and understood. Employee engagement leads to increased productivity and innovation since motivated staff members are more inclined to offer their best ideas and efforts.

Leaders that possess emotional intelligence are also more equipped to handle the complexity and unpredictability of the modern business environment. Leaders who possess the ability to comprehend and regulate their own emotions, along with those of their team members, are more capable of addressing obstacles and transitions. Maintaining organizational performance in the face of quickening technology breakthroughs, changing market conditions, and changing customer expectations requires this flexibility and resilience. Organizations can be set up for long-term success by leaders who can compassionately and strategically lead their teams through these transformations.

Better decision-making is another way that emotional intelligence in leadership benefits a leader. Emotionally intelligent leaders are able to combine emotional and cognitive data to make well-rounded decisions. Leaders are able to make judgments that are ethical, successful, and consistent with the values of their team and company when they take into account both the emotional and rational components of a given scenario. A leader confronted with a challenging business decision, for instance, might think about the possible effects on staff members, clients, and other stakeholders in addition to the financial and strategic ramifications. By taking a comprehensive approach to decision-making, the team and stakeholders' buy-in and trust may be increased, leading to successful implementation and results.

Emotional intelligence also promotes a culture of ongoing education and growth. Leaders that place a high value on emotional intelligence are more inclined to make investments in both their own and their team's development. Leaders may improve the skills and resilience of their teams by fostering a growth attitude and providing chances for learning and development.

This dedication to expansion and improvement is necessary to keep a competitive advantage in the quick-paced, constantly-evolving business world of today.

To sum up, emotional intelligence is an essential part of good leadership. It includes social skills, empathy, self-control, self-awareness, and the capacity to negotiate intricate social dynamics. High emotional intelligence leaders are able to establish a more meaningful connection with their team members, promote a happy and encouraging work atmosphere, and accelerate group performance. Beyond interpersonal relationships, emotional intelligence affects organizational culture, productivity, and long-term success. By putting emotional intelligence first, leaders can position their companies for long-term success by navigating the complexity and unpredictability of today's business climate with empathy, adaptability, and strategic foresight. Emotional intelligence will continue to be a critical competency for leaders who want to motivate, sway opinions, and have a significant impact even as the demands of leadership change.

COMMUNICATION SKILLS

The foundation of successful leadership and an organization is a strong ability to communicate. It is more crucial than ever to be able to communicate effectively, convincingly, and sympathetically in today's fast-paced, connected world. Communication is more than just exchanging information; it's also about developing rapport, understanding, and trust. Teams can be inspired, motivated, and aligned around common goals through effective communication. On the other hand, ineffective communication can result in miscommunication, disputes, and inefficiency. Therefore, anyone who wants to lead and influence others must learn communication skills.

Communication is really about making connections. It is the process by which people communicate their goals, feelings, ideas, and thoughts to other people. This relationship can be established through a variety of channels, including in-person meetings, written communications, formal presentations, and casual discussions. Effective communication demands a clear message, an awareness of the audience, and the capacity to listen and react correctly, regardless of the media.

Clarity is one of the most crucial components of communication. A communication that is easily understood by the recipient is considered clear. This entails speaking clearly and succinctly, staying away from jargon, and being precise with your message. Being clear is especially crucial in leadership, as unclear directives or imprecise criticism can cause misunderstandings and mistakes. A team member might not know exactly what needs to be done if a boss asks them to "improve their performance" without outlining clear goals or rules. Conversely, a precise directive, like "raise your sales by 10% over the next quarter by reaching out to new clients and following up on leads more diligently," offers a well-defined objective and an obvious route to attain it.

Knowing your audience is also necessary for effective communication. Individuals differ in their needs, preferences, and communication styles. A skilled communicator tailors their message to the audience, taking into consideration their emotional condition, knowledge base, and background. When speaking to a non-technical audience, a leader might emphasize the message's wider implications and benefits, but when interacting with a technical team, they might adopt language that is more specific and data-driven. Being attentive to various viewpoints and cognizant of cultural variations is another aspect of understanding the audience. It is essential for successful communication in today's globalized environment, where teams frequently comprise members with diverse cultural backgrounds, to be sensitive to cultural differences.

Another essential part of communication is listening. Although listening is just as vital as speaking, speaking and writing are frequently thought of as the main components of communication. Engaging fully with the speaker, observing their words, tone, and body language, and intelligently replying are all components of active listening. It entails paying attention to what the other person is saying and acting genuinely interested in them. Active listening demonstrates your appreciation for the other person's viewpoint, which fosters rapport and trust. Additionally, it enables you to compile crucial data, clear up misunderstandings, and deliver more pertinent and useful responses. Active listening is a valuable tool for leaders as it may provide valuable insights into team dynamics, identify potential problems, and cultivate a more cooperative and diverse atmosphere.

Empathy is a fundamental component of successful communication and is strongly tied to listening. Empathy is the capacity to comprehend and experience another person's emotions. It enables you to view situations from their point of view and put yourself in their shoes. Developing solid relationships and fostering a positive work environment require this understanding. When a team member is experiencing personal difficulties, for instance, an empathetic leader may offer the required understanding and support, making the team member feel respected and appreciated. Understanding the underlying feelings and motivations of the individuals involved and coming up with solutions that allay their worries are made possible by empathy, which also aids in conflict resolution.

excellent communication also involves excellent nonverbal communication. Our body language, tone of voice, facial expressions, and other nonverbal indicators sometimes transmit more information than words do. These cues have a big impact on how the message is understood and received since they can support or contradict the spoken word. For example, people are more likely to view a leader as trustworthy and authoritative if they talk confidently, keep eye contact, and exhibit open body language. Conversely, a leader who speaks cautiously, avoids making eye contact, and has closed body language could come across as unconfident or untrustworthy. Understanding your own nonverbal cues and how others interpret them will help you communicate more successfully and forge closer bonds with people.

Effective leadership communication also requires the capacity for motivation and inspiration in addition to these fundamental abilities. A leader can inspire greater levels of engagement and performance in their team by effectively communicating a compelling vision and uniting the group around it. This calls for passion and honesty in addition to persuasiveness and clarity. Leaders who communicate with conviction and sincere enthusiasm captivate their listeners and motivate them to act. In this sense, storytelling is a really effective technique. Leaders can increase the relatability and recall of their message by narrating anecdotes that exemplify the organization's vision, values, and objectives. In addition, stories can inspire feelings, give team members a sense of direction, and strengthen their sense of identity.

Another essential component of communication in leadership is feedback. Giving constructive criticism is crucial for development, progress, and learning. But providing feedback well calls for tact and awareness. Feedback ought to be given in a kind and encouraging way, be detailed, and concentrate on behavior rather than the recipient. In order for information to be applicable and useful, it should also be provided promptly, that is, shortly after the incident or behavior in issue. Giving constructive criticism effectively fosters a culture where team members feel free to make errors, grow from them, and keep becoming better. Getting feedback is just as vital. Leaders that are receptive to criticism, actively seek it out, and give constructive criticism show humility and a dedication to their own development. This transparency promotes a mutually respectful and ever-improving culture.

Another area where effective communication is essential is conflict resolution. In every team or organization, disagreements will always arise, but how they are resolved can have a big impact on how things turn out. Conflicts can be transformed into chances for development and innovation with effective communication. This entails listening to all sides concerned, resolving disputes in an open and productive manner, and coming up with just and satisfying solutions. Conflict-resolution experts can handle challenging discussions with tact and sensitivity, ensuring that disputes are settled in a way that fosters cooperation and builds connections.

Leading requires not only communication but also digital landscape navigation. Leaders need to be proficient in using a variety of communication channels, such as email, video conferencing, and instant messaging, given the increase in remote work and digital communication tools. Effective leaders are aware of the advantages and disadvantages of each of these channels and know when to use each one. Routine updates or short queries might be better suited for email or instant messaging, while complex or sensitive topics might be better addressed through a video call or in-person meeting, when nonverbal indications and instant response are accessible. Clarity and conciseness are also necessary in digital communication since messages can be misinterpreted without the context that tone and body language provide. Effective digital communicators are able to forge close bonds with their team members even when they are geographically apart.

Leadership communication also involves the capacity for persuasion and influence. Getting support for their concepts, plans, or choices is often a necessity for leaders. This necessitates both understanding the viewpoints and motivations of the audience in addition to making a logical and persuasive argument. Establishing trust, establishing a common ground, and making an emotional appeal are all necessary for effective persuasion. Effective persuaders may motivate teams, overcome obstacles, and bring them into line with company objectives.

Another essential communication skill for leaders is public speaking. To effectively communicate ideas and motivate action, one must be able to talk clearly and confidently in front of both small and big audiences. Practice, preparation, and the capacity to captivate an audience are necessary for public speaking. To make their message more interesting and remembered, effective public presenters incorporate humor, storytelling, and visual aids. To guarantee that their message is understood, they also pay attention to their pacing, body language, and voice modulation.

To sum up, effective communication is a prerequisite for good leadership. Clarity, audience comprehension, active listening, empathy, nonverbal communication, inspiration, feedback, conflict resolution, digital communication, persuasion, and public speaking are just a few of the skills they cover. With these abilities, leaders may establish rapport with their group, develop trust, encourage cooperation, and propel the success of their company. For leaders who hope to inspire, influence, and leave a lasting impression, developing their communication skills will continue to be essential as the demands of leadership change.

DECISION-MAKING AND PROBLEM-SOLVING

Effective leadership and organizational success are primarily characterized by the possession of critical thinking and problem-solving abilities. These procedures are interdependent, impacting one another, and collectively they serve as the foundation for both operational effectiveness and strategic thinking. Leaders must regularly make deft decisions and apply methodical problem-solving techniques in order to navigate intricate circumstances. An effective way to handle these obstacles can set a successful leader apart from mediocre ones.

Realizing that decision-making is both an art and a science is the first step toward understanding it. It's an art form since it calls for experience, creativity, and intuition. These factors come into play when decision-makers have to make choices without all the knowledge they need or when they have to think creatively to come up with novel solutions. Because it combines data-driven methods, analytical thought, and systematic techniques, decision-making is also a science. Because decision-making is dual in nature, it requires a harmonious fusion of intuitive judgment and logical analysis.

The capacity to recognize and precisely characterize the issue is a fundamental component of good decision-making. This first phase is essential because it creates the framework for identifying the right solution to a well-defined problem. Gathering pertinent data, being aware of the situation, and taking into account the opinions of all parties concerned are requirements for leaders. This thorough comprehension enables leaders to appropriately frame the issue, which in turn directs the following stages of the decision-making process.

The following stage is to come up with possible solutions after the problem has been identified. This stage calls for imagination and receptivity. Proficient leaders promote ideation sessions, cultivate an innovative culture, and embrace a range of viewpoints.

The intention is to generate a wide range of potential solutions without making any snap decisions about their viability. This research stage is crucial for identifying novel concepts and strategies that could otherwise go unnoticed.

Once possible solutions have been identified, executives need to assess them in order to choose the best one. The advantages and disadvantages of each solution are carefully analyzed in this review, taking into account aspects like impact, cost, practicality, and alignment with corporate objectives. Decision matrices, SWOT analysis, and cost-benefit analyses are examples of analytical frameworks and tools that might help in this process. These tools offer an organized method for evaluating the possible results of various options and comparing them. It's crucial to keep in mind, though, that leaders must also use their instincts and judgment in addition to analysis when making a final choice.

The next crucial stage in the decision-making process is putting the selected solution into practice. Thorough planning, unambiguous communication, and efficient implementation are necessary for this phase. A thorough action plan needs to be created, resources must be assigned, roles must be assigned, and deadlines must be set. To make sure that everyone involved understands the choice, their responsibilities, and the anticipated results, communication is essential. Aside from tracking advancement, resolving obstacles, and making the required modifications to stay on course, successful implementation also entails keeping an eye on results.

In addition to following these defined procedures, managing risks and uncertainties is another aspect of decision-making in leadership. Leaders need to be ready to handle uncertainty and change because the corporate environment is frequently unexpected. Identifying possible hazards, evaluating their impact and likelihood, and creating mitigation plans are all part of risk management. This proactive strategy aids in decision-making and helps leaders get ready for any obstacles. Contingency and scenario planning are helpful methods for imagining various future situations and creating adaptable plans of action to deal with them.

Decision-making and problem-solving are closely related abilities that are essential for leaders. Finding a problem's underlying cause, coming up with and assessing several solutions, and successfully putting the selected solution into practice are all parts of problem-solving. Similar to making decisions, fixing problems calls for both inventive and analytical thought.

The first steps in solving an issue effectively are recognizing it and figuring out its root causes. This process entails consulting with stakeholders, assessing data, and compiling pertinent information. In order to find the core reasons of an issue, leaders need to go behind its symptoms. With this increased comprehension, they are able to deal with the issue more deeply and not just cure its symptoms. Leaders can gain a thorough understanding of the problem by delving further into the fundamental causes of the issue with the aid of techniques like the "Five Whys" and root cause analysis.

After the issue is recognized, leaders need to come up with possible fixes. This stage calls for cooperation and inventiveness. Competent leaders foster an atmosphere where team members are at ease expressing their thoughts and viewpoints. Numerous possible solutions can be produced with the aid of collaborative problem-solving methods, design thinking workshops, and brainstorming sessions. Promoting open-mindedness and investigating outlandish concepts that could result in creative solutions is the aim.

A thorough examination of a solution's viability, impact, and alignment with corporate objectives is necessary while evaluating it. Leaders need to think about possible risks and rewards as well as short- and long-term effects. This assessment can benefit from the use of analytical frameworks and methods like impact evaluations, cost-benefit analyses, and decision matrices. But it's crucial to strike a balance between analytical precision and gut feeling. When making decisions, leaders must also take stakeholders' and their organization's values and priorities into account.

Planning, communicating, and carrying out the selected solution effectively are necessary for its implementation. A thorough action plan, resource allocation, and responsibility assignment are all necessary for leaders. To make sure that everyone involved is aware of the plan, their responsibilities, and the anticipated results, clear communication is crucial. In order to stay on course, leaders must also keep an eye on developments, handle any obstacles that crop up, and make the required corrections. Change management is frequently necessary for effective implementation since solutions sometimes call for adjustments to organizational structures, procedures, or behaviors.

Effective communication is essential to the decision-making and problem-solving processes. To make sure that everyone in their team is aware of the issue, the reasoning behind the choice, and the execution strategy, leaders need to speak effectively and persuasively. In addition to fostering a collaborative atmosphere where team members feel appreciated and involved, open and honest communication also creates trust.

Another crucial component of leadership decision-making and problem-solving is empathy. The opinions, requirements, and worries of their stakeholders and team members must be taken into account by leaders. Empathy enables leaders to comprehend how their decisions affect people and create solutions that meet the needs of all stakeholders. This strategy creates a welcoming atmosphere where team members are appreciated and feel heard.

Empathy and emotional intelligence go hand in hand, and emotional intelligence is essential for making wise decisions and solving problems. Emotionally intelligent leaders are conscious of both their own and others' feelings. They are able to effectively control their emotions, maintain composure under duress, and make deliberate choices. Understanding and managing interpersonal connections is another aspect of emotional intelligence that is necessary for fostering teamwork and trust.

Effective decision-making and problem-solving also require resilience and adaptability. The dynamic nature of the business world demands that leaders possess the ability to adjust to novel insights, evolving situations, and unforeseen obstacles. Leaders that are adaptable are receptive to fresh perspectives, flexible in their thinking, and prepared to modify their plans as necessary. Resilience is the capacity to overcome obstacles and keep a positive attitude in the face of difficulty. Resilient leaders can encourage their group to press through and remain committed to their objectives despite adversity.

Apart from these personal attributes and competencies, proficient decision-making and problem-solving necessitate a nurturing company culture. Collaborative, innovative, and continuous improvement-focused cultures encourage a sense of empowerment among team members to share ideas and participate in problem-solving. By setting an example of desired conduct, praising and rewarding contributions, and offering chances for growth and learning, leaders have a significant impact on the culture they create.

Refining decision-making and problem-solving abilities requires ongoing education and training. Leaders need to keep up to date on new technologies and approaches, industry trends, and best practices. They should think back on their experiences, ask their team and other stakeholders for input, and never stop trying to get better at what they do. Opportunities for professional development, such as workshops, mentoring, and training courses, can also assist leaders in improving their capacity for making decisions and solving problems.

In summary, the ability to make decisions and solve problems is essential for effective leadership. Emotional intelligence, creativity, and analytical thinking are all combined in these processes. A thorough grasp of the issue, the creation and assessment of viable alternatives, and the successful application of the selected solution are all necessary for making decisions and solving problems effectively. In addition, excellent communication, risk and uncertainty management, empathy, flexibility, and resilience are required of leaders. These abilities are additionally strengthened by an encouraging corporate culture and a dedication to lifelong learning and growth. Leaders may effectively traverse complex issues, propel corporate achievement, and leave a lasting impression by developing their decision-making and problem-solving skills.

BUILDING CONFIDENCE AND PRESENCE

Establishing presence and confidence is essential to good leadership. While presence demands respect and builds trust, confidence gives leaders the ability to make bold decisions and take calculated risks. These characteristics work together to produce a captivating personality that motivates and inspires people. Gaining self-assurance and presence is not only advantageous, but also necessary in a society where leaders must constantly navigate difficulties and scrutiny.

Self-awareness is the first step on the path to developing presence and confidence. It takes understanding one's ideals, strengths, and shortcomings to be a genuine leader. Leaders that are self-aware are able to address their weaknesses and successfully utilize their assets. Additionally, it guarantees that their choices and actions are consistent with their basic beliefs, fostering authenticity and consistency in their leadership style. Building presence requires authenticity since it cultivates respect and trust among stakeholders and team members.

Self-awareness can grow as a result of introspection and criticism. Reflection is devoting time to in-depth thought of one's past experiences, decisions, and results. It necessitates an open evaluation of what succeeded, what failed, and why. Through this approach, leaders can improve their decision-making going forward by learning from their past mistakes. Contrarily, feedback offers an outside viewpoint on one's actions and output. Getting input from dependable coworkers, mentors, and team members can give important insights into your strengths and places for development. Additionally, it shows a dedication to improvement, which fosters respect and trust.

Competence is another essential component in developing confidence. Knowledge and abilities gained through education and experience are frequently the foundation of confidence. Leaders who possess competence feel more confident about their ability to meet and overcome obstacles. Through ongoing education and training, this competency is developed. Leaders need to keep up to date on new technologies and approaches, industry trends, and best practices. They ought to look for chances for continuing education, such as seminars, coaching, and training courses. Acquiring proficiency in their domain not only increases their self-assurance but also amplifies their legitimacy and visibility.

Another key component of confidence building is preparation. For meetings, presentations, and decision-making procedures, being well-prepared makes leaders feel more assured and enhances their performance. Getting ready entails assembling pertinent data, foreseeing probable queries and difficulties, and organizing answers. It also entails practicing important points and delivery strategies. Leaders who are well-prepared can make their points more effectively and convincingly, which improves their presence.

Additionally essential to gaining confidence is resilience. Since the corporate world is frequently unpredictable, leaders need to be able to overcome obstacles and setbacks with a positive outlook. The capacity to recover from setbacks, grow from errors, and preserve optimism are all parts of resilience. Resilient leaders reassure their team and inspire trust in their abilities by demonstrating their ability to overcome hardship. Adopting a growth mindset—in which obstacles are perceived as chances for learning and development rather than as threats—is essential to building resilience. It also necessitates self-care and stress-reduction strategies including exercise, mindfulness, and preserving a positive work-life balance.

Another essential element of presence and confidence is emotional intelligence. Emotionally intelligent leaders are conscious of both their own and others' feelings. They are able to properly control their emotions, maintain composure under duress, and forge solid bonds with others. Leaders that possess emotional intelligence are better able to handle social difficulties, settle disputes, and encourage and inspire their group. It calls for social skills, self-control, and empathy. Emotionally intelligent leaders improve their presence and impact at work by fostering a supportive and upbeat atmosphere.

Additionally necessary for establishing presence and confidence is effective communication. Leaders need to be able to communicate their views convincingly and with clarity. This encompasses both the message's substance and its delivery. With the right body language, eye contact, and vocal intonation, confident leaders communicate with clarity and conviction. Additionally, they listen intently, expressing a sincere interest in the viewpoints of others and giving intelligent answers. Building rapport and trust via effective communication is essential to presence. It also guarantees that the team members fully comprehend and support the leader's vision and objectives.

One particular area of communication that is crucial for developing presence is public speaking. Whether in team meetings, conferences, or open forums, leaders frequently have to speak in front of sizable crowds. Confidence and the capacity to captivate and motivate an audience are prerequisites for public speaking. You can get better at this ability by training and practicing. Taking public speaking classes or joining clubs like Toastmasters can offer helpful practice and criticism. Proficient orators employ narrative techniques, levity, and graphic aids to enhance the impact and retention of their speech. To guarantee that their message is understood, they also pay attention to their pacing, body language, and voice modulation.

An further essential component of presence is authenticity. Real leaders stay loyal to who they are and what they believe in. When it comes to their choices and acts, they are open, truthful, and reliable. Since team members and stakeholders can see that a leader is acting in accordance with their words, authenticity fosters a sense of mutual respect and trust. In addition, sincere leaders foster an environment where team members feel free to voice their opinions and concerns. The leader's presence is enhanced by this authenticity since it encourages sincere bonds and loyalty.

Taking chances and venturing outside of one's comfort zone are further components of developing presence and confidence. Leaders need to be prepared to take on novel tasks, reach tough choices, and work toward lofty objectives. This courage to take chances shows self-assurance in one's skills and encourages others to follow suit. It also offers chances for development and education. Risk-takers and experience-seekers develop resilience and adaptability, which bolsters their presence and self-assurance.

Developing presence and confidence can also be greatly aided by mentoring and role models. Gaining knowledge and direction from seasoned leaders is quite beneficial. Mentors can be a source of guidance, support, and encouragement by sharing their experiences. Leaders might be motivated to adopt successful behaviors and tactics by watching role models. Creating a network of role models and mentors may offer continuous guidance and educational opportunities, assisting leaders in enhancing their self-assurance and visibility.

Establishing a welcoming and encouraging work atmosphere is crucial for boosting self-esteem and presence. Leaders need to promote a culture of cooperation, acknowledgment, and ongoing development. Team members are more inclined to offer their best efforts and ideas when they feel appreciated and supported. The ability of the leader to inspire and motivate their team is reflected in this favorable environment, which amplifies their presence. By praising and celebrating accomplishments, offering helpful criticism, and promoting candid dialogue and teamwork, leaders may foster this atmosphere.

Another crucial component of developing presence and confidence is delegation. Good leaders understand that they are not able to handle every task on their own. They need to be able to assign duties and obligations to other members of their team. By empowering team members to accept responsibility for their job, delegation demonstrates trust in the skills of others. Leaders are also able to concentrate on higher-level decision-making and strategic concerns. Effective delegation enables leaders to assemble a capable and powerful team, enhancing their visibility and impact.

Developing presence and confidence also requires practicing mindfulness and self-care. Leaders need to look after their mental, emotional, and physical health. This entails preserving a positive work-life balance, engaging in stress-reduction and mindfulness practices, and setting aside time for relaxation and renewal. Leaders who have had enough sleep and maintain a healthy balance are more alert, focused, and productive. Deep breathing exercises and other mindfulness techniques can also help leaders remain composed under pressure and improve their presence.

Building presence and confidence requires not just these specific exercises but also continual learning and growth. Leaders need to keep up to date on new technologies and approaches, industry trends, and best practices. They ought to look for chances for continuing education, such as seminars, coaching, and training courses. Leaders who engage in ongoing learning and development are certain to maintain their competence and self-assurance. It also shows a dedication to development and quality, which strengthens their presence even more.

To sum up, developing presence and confidence is crucial for effective leadership. These attributes enable leaders to take calculated chances, make snap decisions, and motivate and inspire others. A mix of self-awareness, competence, readiness, resilience, emotional intelligence, effective communication, authenticity, taking risks, mentoring, positive work settings, delegation, mindfulness, and ongoing learning is needed to develop presence and confidence. Leaders may establish a captivating character that inspires trust, commands respect, and propels organizational success by honing these abilities and behaviors.

CHAPTER 4

THE LEADERSHIP ACT

LEADING BY EXAMPLE

One of the most potent and persistent tenets of effective leadership is setting a good example. Based on the straightforward yet deep idea that deeds speak louder than words, it cuts across sectors, cultural boundaries, and historical periods. The conduct of a leader sets the standard for the entire group, impacting everyone's attitudes, deeds, and output. Leaders foster loyalty, trust, and respect by modeling the behaviors and standards they expect from their people. This chapter examines the many facets of setting a good example, highlighting its significance and applicability via case studies from the past and present.

The first step in comprehending the core of leading by example is realizing that being a leader involves more than just giving orders or exercising authority. It has to do with responsibility, honesty, and influence. A culture of excellence and moral conduct is instilled in organizations by leaders who embody these attributes. This idea dates back to antiquity, when leaders such as Alexander the Great showed the value of setting a good example. Alexander was renowned for walking with his warriors and going through the same struggles as them.

His troops' strong sense of devotion and allegiance was cultivated by this cohesion, which helped explain his many military victories.

Mahatma Gandhi's life is a powerful example of leading by example in more recent history. Gandhi inspired millions of people to fight for India's independence with his nonviolent resistance philosophy and his own dedication to self-discipline and humble living. His steadfast commitment to his cause was evidenced by his readiness to suffer hardship and imprisonment in order to uphold his ideas. Gandhi's example of moral leadership and nonviolent resistance inspired a nation and created a long-lasting legacy.

In the business world, setting a good example is just as important. Take the example of Herb Kelleher, the former CEO and co-founder of Southwest Airlines. Kelleher was renowned for his genuine concern for his staff members and his hands-on leadership approach. He handled bags and served customers frequently while working with front-line employees. Within the organization, a strong sense of camaraderie and mutual respect were built by this outward display of dedication and humility. Kelleher's strategy contributed to the development of a cooperative and customer-focused culture that was essential to Southwest Airlines' success.

Mary Barra is another outstanding businesswoman and CEO of General Motors. Barra's ascent to the top of a male-dominated field is impressive, but what really makes her stand out as a leader is her approach to it. Barra gained notoriety for being open and responsible, especially during the GM ignition switch debacle. Rather than assigning blame, she accepted accountability, revised the organization's safety procedures, and sought to restore confidence among stakeholders and customers. Her deeds exhibited a dedication to honesty and responsibility, highlighting the significance of these principles across the entire company.

Setting a good example also entails being open to innovation and change. Apple co-founder Steve Jobs was a prime example of this idea. Jobs contributed significantly to the conception and advancement of Apple's products in addition to being a visionary. His zeal for innovation and his unwavering pursuit of excellence established high standards for his staff. Apple rose to the top of the technology sector thanks to Jobs' dedication to designing devices that are both aesthetically beautiful and easy to use. The company's success is attributed to the creative and innovative culture he built through his leadership by example.

Leading by example is a striking illustration of Malala Yousafzai's approach to social advocacy. Malala persisted in her battle for girls' education rights even after she was shot by the Taliban for doing so. Her bravery and tenacity in the face of overwhelming tragedy have motivated people all throughout the world. Malala's selfless giving and constant dedication to her cause are prime examples of the significant influence of setting a good example. Her activities have not only increased awareness of the problem of girls' education on a global scale but have also given many people the confidence to advocate for their rights.

Within the realm of sports, there is also clear leadership by example. Throughout his career, Michael Jordan— who is frequently considered to be among the best basketball players of all time—exemplified this idea. Jordan's unwavering commitment to excellence, competitive nature, and unwavering work ethic set a high bar for his teammates. Beyond his on-court accomplishments, he inspired others with his dedication to training, his unwavering focus, and his refusal to accept mediocrity. Jordan's leadership helped create the Chicago Bulls' culture, which helped him win six NBA titles and solidify his reputation as a sports icon.

Nelson Mandela's life and leadership style serve as a powerful example of leading by example in the context of public service. Throughout his life, Mandela demonstrated a strong commitment to justice, equality, and reconciliation via his acts. Mandela was released from prison after 27 years, bearing a message of peace and forgiveness. His leadership during South Africa's transition from apartheid to democracy showed how deeply he believed in peace and tolerance. Mandela gained respect and affection throughout the world for his ability to lead by example and exhibit grace and wisdom in the face of overwhelming adversity.

Setting an example for others is a concept that may be used in everyday life and in a variety of situations; it is not just reserved for well-known leaders or significant historical people. For example, teachers set an example for their pupils when they are passionate about what they teach, treat them with respect, and live according to the ideals of curiosity and lifelong learning. Parents mold their children's character and beliefs by setting an example through their acts and behaviors. When volunteers and community leaders give freely of their time and resources to causes they support, they set an example for others to follow and encourage them to join them.

Setting a good example has many benefits. First of all, it increases credibility and confidence. Leaders gain the trust of their followers when they regularly exhibit the attitudes and actions that they promote. Effective leadership is built on trust because it encourages candid communication, teamwork, and a willingness to follow. When leaders are perceived as sincere and dependable, their credibility is further increased. Leaders who demonstrate exemplary behavior are more likely to be respected and supported by their followers.

Second, inspiring and motivating others comes from setting an example. It is human nature for people to want to act and behave like the people they look up to. When leaders exhibit commitment, resiliency, and moral conduct, they motivate others to hold themselves to the same standards. Higher levels of performance, morale, and involvement within an organization can result from this inspiration. A leader's good example has the power to change an organization's culture and spur group success.

Furthermore, setting a good example encourages a sense of responsibility and accountability. Leaders who hold themselves to a high standard encourage others to follow suit. People adopt a culture of accountability as a result, accepting responsibility for their deeds and results. Team members are more likely to hold one another and themselves accountable in such a setting, which promotes moral behavior and better performance.

In times of crisis, the idea of setting a good example is also quite important. Followers look to their leaders for direction and comfort during trying times. In times of crisis, leaders who maintain composure, fortitude, and a solution-focused mindset instill stability and confidence. Their actions set the standard for how the company handles hardship. This was seen during the COVID-19 epidemic, when leaders were able to lead their organizations through previously unheard-of obstacles by exhibiting empathy, transparency, and swift action.

Take Jacinda Ardern, the prime minister of New Zealand, as an example during the pandemic. Ardern gained the respect and confidence of many people by acting decisively and communicating with empathy. Setting a good example, she made difficult decisions to safeguard the public's health while displaying compassion and fortitude. Her leadership approach helped New Zealanders feel a feeling of shared responsibility and togetherness, which helped the nation respond to the crisis effectively.

Setting a good example requires ongoing education and improvement. Proficient leaders acknowledge their limitations and the constant need for improvement. Leaders inspire their staff to embrace a lifelong learning and self-improvement mindset by setting an example. In today's world of rapid change, innovation and adaptability are critical for long-term success, and this culture of continual learning fosters both.

Within the tech sector, Microsoft CEO Satya Nadella is a prime example of this strategy. Nadella has changed Microsoft's culture since taking over by placing a strong emphasis on ongoing learning and a growth attitude. His exemplary leadership, which emphasizes empathy, teamwork, and creativity, has revitalized the business and set it up for long-term success. Nadella's staff members are motivated to embrace change and strive for greatness by his openness to learning and adapting.

Integrity and moral behavior are additional aspects of leading by example. Leaders frequently have to make morally challenging choices. People who continuously decide to act honorably—even in difficult or unpopular situations—set a tremendous example for others. A culture of trust and integrity is created by ethical leadership, giving team members the assurance that they work for a company that respects and adheres to moral principles.

The case of Paul Polman, the former CEO of Unilever, serves as an example. Polman is renowned for his dedication to ethical and ecological business methods. He promoted the Unilever Sustainable Living Plan during his time there, which aims to lessen the company's negative environmental effects and improve its good social impacts. By setting an example of sustainability and ethics above earnings in the near term, Polman encouraged other businesses to follow suit and proved that moral leadership can lead to long-term success.

Setting a good example for pupils is essential in education as it helps mold their minds and morals. Teachers who exhibit a love of learning, an appreciation for variety, and a dedication to quality encourage their pupils to embrace these ideals. For example, the well-known high school math instructor Jaime Escalante is well-known for his work with East Los Angeles's impoverished children. Escalante changed many people's lives and produced amazing academic results because of his commitment, high standards, and faith in his pupils' abilities. His exemplary leadership showed the significant influence that teachers can have on the lives of their students.

To sum up, setting a good example for others to follow is a timeless and generally applicable fundamental of effective leadership. It is based on the idea that deeds speak louder than words and crosses industries and situations. Leaders inspire people, create a culture of responsibility and excellence, and establish trust by modeling the attitudes and actions they want to see in others. Examples from the past and present, such as Gandhi and Jacinda Ardern, demonstrate the transformational power of setting a good example. This idea continues to be the cornerstone of moral and successful leadership, directing leaders to bring about progressive and long-lasting change in every field of endeavor—business, education, public service, or daily life.

CREATING VISION AND MISSION

A vital job for any leader who wants to motivate and steer his organization toward long-term success is developing a vision and mission. An organization's vision paints a vivid picture of the future and the goal it hopes to achieve. Conversely, the mission statement outlines the organization's goals, the reason it exists, and the fundamental principles that direct its operations. When combined, these components act as a North Star, directing the activities of all organization members and guaranteeing that they are all working toward the same objective. This chapter explores the complexities of developing a vision and mission statement, highlighting the significance of these statements with in-depth case studies of well-known individuals and institutions.

Understanding the larger environment in which the company functions and engaging in introspection are the first steps in developing a vision. Often called a SWOT analysis, it entails a thorough examination of the organization's advantages, disadvantages, opportunities, and threats. Using this technique, leaders can find the special skills and possible growth areas that will help them reach their desired future state. Furthermore, a vision need to be aspirational, pushing the company to pursue excellence while staying realistic and attainable.

Steve Jobs of Apple is among the most recognizable figures in visionary leadership. Jobs was back at Apple in 1997, but the firm was in trouble, its product line was disorganized, and its finances were getting worse. Jobs had a very clear vision: to make things that improve people's lives by using inventive and beautiful design. This concept aimed to make technology an extension of the human experience, not just a means to make money. The creation and introduction of ground-breaking devices like the iPod, iPhone, and iPad, which completely changed sectors and established Apple as a leader in innovation, were striking examples of Steve Jobs' vision.

The ability to clearly and powerfully articulate Jobs' vision was crucial in uniting Apple's partners, consumers, and staff under a single objective. His ability to look above the problems at hand and imagine a time when design and technology would effortlessly converge defined a direction that Apple is still going today. This vision was successful not just in how it was expressed but also in how hard it was pursued, proving how important vision is to the success of a business.

Elon Musk's plans for SpaceX offer yet another striking illustration. Musk established SpaceX with the goal of facilitating space travel and eventually settling on Mars. His conviction that humanity needs to live on multiple planets in order to survive inspired this bold concept. A new era of space exploration, characterized by advancements like reusable rockets and private space travel, has been spurred by Musk's ambition for SpaceX. The company's accomplishments, which include the building of the Starship spaceship and successful visits to the International Space Station, are proof of the potency of an audacious and revolutionary vision.

But a vision can only be successful if it is supported by a goal that is both distinct and focused. The organization's core goals and guiding principles are summarized in the mission statement. It responds to the queries: What makes us human? What values do we uphold? A strong mission statement serves as the cornerstone for strategic planning and decision-making, guaranteeing that every action is in line with the goals and basic values of the company.

The outdoor clothing brand Patagonia provides a notable illustration of a firm that is driven by its mission.

Patagonia's motto, "We're in business to save our home planet," sums up the company's dedication to ethical corporate conduct and environmental sustainability. The company's operations, including its corporate philanthropy and supply chain procedures, have been directed by this objective. Initiatives like the Worn Wear program, which encourages customers to repair and recycle their gear, and the company's dedication to using organic and recycled materials demonstrate Patagonia's attention on sustainability. In addition to helping the business stand out in a crowded industry, the company's mission has attracted a devoted following of clients who share its beliefs.

TOMS Shoes is a potent illustration of an organization with a clear aim. The goal of Blake Mycoskie's startup company, TOMS, is to improve lives via business. The business's "One for One" strategy, which donates a pair of shoes for each pair sold, has had a significant positive influence on local communities all around the world. Millions of shoes have been given to underprivileged children thanks to this mission-driven strategy, which has also encouraged other businesses to use comparable social impact strategies. The core of TOMS' brand identity is its mission, which appeals to customers who wish to use their purchases to change the world.

It takes more than just mental clarity to create a vision and mission—effective communication of these ideas is also necessary. It is imperative for leaders to effectively communicate their vision and objective to all relevant parties, such as partners, consumers, employees, and investors. This entails developing an engaging story that links the objectives of the organization with the hopes and ideals of its constituents. Everyone will understand and be inspired to contribute to the long-term success of the company if there is effective communication.

The leadership of Howard Schultz at Starbucks serves as an example of how important good communication is in reiterating a company's vision and goals. In addition to being a coffee shop, Schultz saw Starbucks as a "third place" where people could unwind and socialize in between their homes and places of employment. A mission to uplift and nourish the human spirit, one person, one cup, and one neighborhood at a time, was added to this vision. Through every facet of the company, from customer service and shop design to ethical sourcing and staff benefits, Schultz conveyed this vision and objective. The company's vision and mission were effectively communicated and embodied by him, resulting in a powerful, values-driven brand that attracted attention from all around the world.

Engaging stakeholders in the process of developing a vision and purpose helps to guarantee that their viewpoints and goals are taken into account. The adoption of a collaborative approach among stakeholders cultivates a sense of ownership and commitment, so increasing the likelihood of their support and participation in the vision and mission. There are many ways to involve stakeholders, including focus groups, surveys, open forums, and workshops. The knowledge acquired from these exchanges can be a great asset in developing an ambitious vision and goal that is firmly based in the circumstances of the business.

The time that Indra Nooyi spent as PepsiCo's CEO offers a striking illustration of how stakeholders can be included in the process of developing a vision and mission. In order to achieve sustainable growth, Nooyi introduced the idea of "Performance with Purpose," which called for making investments in a better future for both the earth and humankind. Several conversations with stakeholders, including customers, workers, investors, and others, went into creating this vision. By interacting with stakeholders, Nooyi made sure that the company's vision reflected their expectations and values, which in turn helped to build widespread support for the company's strategic ambitions. PepsiCo undertook advances in community development, sustainability, and healthier product creation under her direction, showcasing the effectiveness of a vision and mission driven by stakeholder engagement.

Developing a vision and mission statement necessitates ongoing improvement and alignment with the organization's changing environment. To make sure that the vision and mission are still applicable and motivating, leaders must periodically review and, if needed, update them. This continuous process entails asking stakeholders for input, evaluating organizational performance, and keeping an eye on outside developments. Leaders can guarantee that the vision and goal remain a compass for the organization's path by remaining aware of changes in both the environment and the organization.

Microsoft's development under Satya Nadella serves as an example. Nadella outlined a new goal for Microsoft when he was appointed CEO in 2014: "to empower every person and every organization on the planet to achieve more." The company's prior concentration on a "devices and services" approach was replaced with a broader focus on cloud computing, artificial intelligence, and digital transformation with the release of this vision. Nadella also adjusted Microsoft's mission statement, which was to "empower every person and every organization on the planet to achieve more," to better reflect the new direction. Microsoft has experienced substantial growth and innovation as a result of this strategy realignment, establishing it as a leader in the technology sector.

IBM under Ginni Rometty is another illustration of how vision and mission have evolved. Under Rometty's direction, IBM changed from being a hardware-focused business to a leader in blockchain, cloud computing, and AI. "Cognitive solutions and cloud platform" was the vision she presented, and it complemented IBM's objective to "help clients transform, innovate, and grow." IBM's key initiatives, such as the acquisition of Red Hat and the creation of Watson AI, were directed by its vision and mission. IBM was able to reposition itself for future success in large part because to Rometty's ability to modify the vision and mission to reflect the rapidly evolving technology world.

Realistic and ambitious goals must be balanced in order to create a vision and mission. A vision needs to be realistic in addition to being difficult and ambitious. Unattainable goals can alienate and depress participants, which can result in annoyance and a loss of trust. Inspiring their organization to achieve new heights while making sure the vision is based on the organization's resources and capabilities requires leaders to strike a balance. Maintaining motivation and momentum in the direction of realizing the vision depends on this balance.

The Bill and Melinda Gates Foundation is an illustration of how to strike a balance between ambition and practicality in the nonprofit sector. The mission statement of the foundation is "a world where every person has the opportunity to live a healthy, productive life." The mission statement is, "work with partners to tackle critical problems primarily in the areas of health, education, and poverty." This is an ambitious vision that is being pursued. Within its mission areas, which include promoting access to education and eradicating diseases like polio, the foundation establishes clear, quantifiable targets. The Gates Foundation has significantly advanced toward its objectives and had a major impact on global health and development by striking a balance between its aspirational vision and practical, evidence-based initiatives.

The process of developing a vision and mission requires reflection, participation, communication, and adaptation. It is dynamic and iterative. It is an essential responsibility for leaders who want to motivate and steer their companies toward sustained success. We are shown the transforming potential of a clear and compelling vision and mission by the following examples: Satya Nadella, Elon Musk, Indra Nooyi, Satya Nadella, Steve Jobs, and the Bill and Melinda Gates Foundation. These leaders have shown that a clear goal and vision can motivate people to take action, coordinate efforts, and produce noteworthy results.

To sum up, developing a vision and purpose statement is essential to good leadership. It calls for a thorough comprehension of the background of the business, a cooperative approach to engaging stakeholders, and the capacity to successfully convey and embodies the vision and mission. Leaders need to strike a balance between aspiration and practicality, review and improve their vision and mission on a regular basis, and make sure these tenets are still motivating and relevant. By doing this, they may provide their organization a feeling of direction and purpose that inspires and unites them and propels them toward success and impact in the future.

INSPIRING AND MOTIVATING OTHERS

Among the many attributes that set exceptional leaders apart in the field of leadership, inspiring and motivating others is one that sticks out. It is both an art and a science to be able to instill passion, drive, and dedication in a group of people or an organization; it takes a profound grasp of human nature, skillful communication, and sincere empathy. The complexities of inspiring and motivating others are examined in this chapter, which is enhanced with real-world case studies showing how effective leaders have used these abilities to produce outstanding results.

Gaining a deep understanding of the people you want to lead is the first step towards inspiring and encouraging others. This comprehension explores their goals, anxieties, abilities, and shortcomings in addition to their names and occupations. A connection that goes beyond transactional contacts is made by leaders who are able to access these personal qualities. They provide each person a feeling of purpose and belonging, making them feel important and essential to the group's goal.

Take Nelson Mandela as an example. His leadership both during and after his incarceration serves as a powerful source of inspiration and motivation. Mandela's goal of a democratic and racially peaceful South Africa was a deeply personal purpose in addition to his political one. Mandela served 27 years in prison, but he came out of it without resentment, prepared to guide his country toward peace. His remarkable ability to relate to people from all walks of life, along with his persistent devotion to justice and equality, were the main sources of his inspiration. Millions were inspired to cooperate in pursuit of a common objective by Mandela's speeches, deeds, and overall message of hope and togetherness.

Mandela's sincerity and moral character served as the foundation for his method of motivating people. He set an exemplary example for others to follow, exhibiting forbearance, resiliency, and an unwavering faith in the potential for change. Even his old opponents were moved by his openness to interact with his opponents and his appeal for forgiveness rather than retaliation, which demonstrated moral leadership. This instance emphasizes how crucial authenticity is in leadership; followers are motivated by sincere leaders who uphold the principles they preach.

Within the corporate sector, Howard Schultz's management at Starbucks offers yet another potent example of encouraging and inspiring people. In addition to selling coffee, Schultz wanted Starbucks to become a "third place" where people could socialize and unwind in between their homes and places of employment. Inspired by the strength of community and by Schultz's own experiences, this idea was intensely personal. He was passionate about sharing this vision with his staff, whom he called "partners," highlighting their pivotal role in crafting the Starbucks experience.

Schultz's dedication to his team's welfare demonstrated his capacity to motivate them. He introduced stock options and full health insurance for part-timers, which is uncommon in the service sector. Schultz promoted a culture of loyalty and drive by making investments in his staff and showing them respect and consideration. His efforts fostered a sense of unity and belonging among his staff members by demonstrating his regard for them as people in addition to their roles as employees.

Being able to articulate a compelling vision is essential for inspiring and motivating people. This vision serves as a beacon, directing the company and providing context for the difficulties and daily activities that it faces. The famous "I Have a Dream" speech by Martin Luther King Jr. epitomizes the impact of a compelling vision. Millions of people were captivated by King's brilliant description of his vision for an equitable and racially integrated society. A generation was motivated to act by his ability to present a compelling vision of the future and to emphasize the importance of justice, equality, and freedom.

King's systematic approach to activism demonstrated his leadership qualities, which extended beyond his oratory prowess. He realized that motivating people needed more than simply an emotional hook; it also needed a well-defined plan and attainable objectives. King's ability to blend motivational speech with efficient mobilization and planning contributed to the success of the Civil Rights Movement. Through his leadership, he showed that while a captivating vision can arouse emotion, in order to retain momentum and inspire sustained action, it must be backed by doable milestones and realistic initiatives.

Within the sports domain, the leadership of the renowned NBA coach Phil Jackson provides insightful knowledge about inspiring and motivating teams. Jackson was renowned for his distinctive coaching method, which combined mindfulness, psychology, and a thorough understanding of team dynamics. He coached the Chicago Bulls and Los Angeles Lakers to several titles. Jackson had a holistic approach, emphasizing his players' mental and emotional health in addition to their athletic prowess.

A fundamental tactic employed by Jackson was fostering a feeling of cohesion and shared objectives. He popularized the idea of the "triangle offense," a scheme that prioritized responsibility and cooperation among team members. Jackson inspired his players to help one another and strive toward shared objectives by creating a culture that valued individual talent within the framework of team accomplishment. His ability to instill confidence and faith in his players allowed them to push themselves to new heights and accomplish excellence as a team under his leadership.

Jackson's emphasis on presence and mindfulness was yet another essential component of his inspirational leadership style. In order to help his players handle stress and keep their composure under duress, he urged them to meditate and to concentrate on the here and now. Their on-court performance was enhanced by this strategy, which also encouraged personal development and resiliency. Jackson's leadership style serves as an example of how crucial it is to attend to people's complete needs in order to effectively inspire and motivate them.

One of the best examples of how to inspire and motivate people in the corporate world is Satya Nadella's makeover of Microsoft. Microsoft was experiencing a lack of innovation and a stagnating culture when Nadella took over as CEO in 2014. In addition to outlining a vision that is focused on "empowering every person and every organization on the planet to achieve more," Nadella stressed the significance of a growth mindset, or the conviction that skills can be acquired by commitment and diligence.

Nadella's inclusiveness and empathy were hallmarks of his leadership. He placed a high value on knowing the viewpoints of his staff members and listening to them in order to promote an environment of candid dialogue and teamwork. Through his emphasis on ongoing education and growth, Nadella encouraged his staff members to be adaptable and take chances. His focus on growth and empathy fostered a culture where everyone felt appreciated and inspired to give their all.

Another important point made by Nadella's leadership was how crucial it is to match the organization's beliefs and mission. Under his direction, Microsoft made investments in accessibility technology and reduced its carbon footprint as part of its commitment to moral behavior and social responsibility. Employee and consumer dedication to the company's objectives was strengthened by this alignment of purpose and values. Nadella's leadership exemplifies that a clear vision, a culture of support, and a dedication to values that are shared by stakeholders are necessary for inspiring and motivating people.

Malala Yousafzai is a remarkable example of inspirational and motivating leadership, and her life and work are worth studying. Malala has inspired millions of people worldwide with her support of girls' education against overwhelming difficulties. With even more vigor, Malala pursued her battle for education after escaping a Taliban attack on her life. She has become a universal representation of the strength of youth and the value of education due to her bravery, tenacity, and unshakable dedication to her cause.

Malala's genuineness and her intimate ties to the causes she supports are what make her an inspiration to others. Her writings and speeches exude a profound empathy for the causes she supports, and people of many backgrounds can relate to her personal narrative. Malala has crafted a compelling story by sharing her struggles and experiences, inspiring people to take up the cause of educational justice. Her example serves as a powerful reminder of the value of genuine connection and personal connection in inspiring and encouraging others.

Within the nonprofit sector, Bill and Melinda Gates' foundational leadership provides a powerful example of inspiring and encouraging others to take on global concerns. With a better world in mind for all, the Gates Foundation works to enhance healthcare, combat poverty, and provide access to education. Through the use of their money and influence, Bill and Melinda Gates have been able to increase support for programs including boosting access to education, eradicating diseases, and improving sanitation.

Their dedication to teamwork and data-driven methodology define their leadership. Other stakeholders have shown faith and investment in the Gates Foundation by setting clear goals and tracking progress. In order to accomplish their goals, Bill and Melinda

Gates also stress the value of partnerships, collaborating with communities, organizations, and governments. Their strategic vision, evidence-based methodology, and dedication to creating a real impact are the foundations of their capacity to uplift and encourage others.

Acknowledging and applauding accomplishments is another way to inspire and motivate people. Leaders who celebrate their team members' accomplishments and efforts help to create a supportive and encouraging environment. This acknowledgement can come in a variety of forms, such as thank-you notes and rewards given either in public or privately. Honoring successes not only raises spirits but also serves to reinforce the attitudes and practices that make the company successful.

Within the field of education, Jaime Escalante, a math teacher in a high school, is a prime example of how kids can be motivated by praise and recognition. Escalante's work with East Los Angeles' impoverished pupils gained notoriety thanks to the movie "Stand and Deliver." His pupils were challenged to take and do well in Advanced Placement Calculus because he had high expectations for them. Escalante's tough instruction and encouragement, along with his faith in his pupils' abilities, produced outstanding academic results.

Escalante's capacity to acknowledge and applaud his pupils' accomplishments was a defining quality of his leadership. He established an environment of excellence where achievement and diligence were valued. Escalante inspired his students to strive for greater things by acknowledging and applauding their accomplishments. His example of leadership showed how acknowledging and applauding achievements may motivate others to go above and beyond their own goals and become great.

The inventor and host of "Mister Rogers' Neighborhood," Fred Rogers, offers a distinctive viewpoint on inspiring and motivating people when it comes to community leadership. Rogers had a significant influence on many generations of viewers with his kind and compassionate attitude to children's programming. He made every youngster feel respected and understood by sensitively and carefully addressing difficult emotional and social difficulties.

Rogers' genuine concern and regard for his audience were the foundation of his inspirational and motivating speeches. He inspired a sense of self-worth and belonging in his audience by spreading themes of love, acceptance, and kindness. Rogers' leadership serves as an example of how compassion and a strong dedication to the welfare of others can lead to inspiration and drive.

To sum up, encouraging and motivating people is a complex task that calls for a strong grasp of human nature, clear communication, honesty, empathy, and a dedication to moral principles. Leaders can inspire and motivate those they lead in a variety of ways, as demonstrated by the lives of Nelson Mandela, Howard Schultz, Martin Luther King Jr., Phil Jackson, Satya Nadella, Malala Yousafzai, Bill and Melinda Gates, Jaime Escalante, and Fred Rogers. These leaders have demonstrated that inspiring and motivating others is a universal skill that can spur positive change and lead to extraordinary results, regardless of the industry or setting. They have exemplified the transforming potential of inspirational leadership via their vision, deeds, and interpersonal relationships.

DELEGATION AND EMPOWERMENT

Empowerment and delegation are essential elements of good leadership and are essential to developing a motivated and effective staff. Fundamentally, these ideas are about assigning people jobs and granting them the freedom and power to complete them. This builds a sense of ownership and dedication while also utilizing the team's combined abilities. This chapter examines the nuances of empowerment and delegation, highlighting their significance with in-depth case studies of well-known individuals and institutions.

In its most basic form, delegation is when a leader assigns duties or responsibilities to their subordinates. This method involves more than just assigning work; it also involves identifying each team member's special talents and abilities and matching tasks to them. Understanding the skills, goals, and developmental requirements of each team member is essential for effective delegation. Leaders can guarantee that the proper people are working on the right tasks and boost productivity and efficiency by assigning jobs appropriately.

On the other hand, empowerment involves more than just assigning responsibilities. It entails giving people the power, means, and autonomy to decide what to do and how to do it within their spheres of responsibility. Not only can empowered workers do tasks, but they also make decisions and come up with new ideas. Employee initiative, experimentation, and innovative contribution to the organization's objectives are all encouraged when they feel trusted and empowered.

Sir Richard Branson, the creator of the Virgin Group, is a prime illustration of empowerment and delegation in action. Branson is well-known for his decentralized management approach, which places a strong emphasis on accountability and autonomy. The Virgin Group consists of more than 400 separate businesses that run on their own. According to Branson, delegation entails choosing qualified executives for each firm and granting them the latitude to manage their operations as they see right.

The foundation of Branson's thinking is his conviction that an organization's most valuable resource is its workforce—talented and driven individuals. He guarantees that his managers have the freedom to innovate and adjust to shifting market conditions by giving them authority and giving them the tools they need. Virgin's ability to enter and flourish in a variety of industries, including music, telecommunications, and airlines, has been greatly aided by this strategy. Empowered leaders are more willing to take measured risks and investigate new prospects, as demonstrated by Branson's leadership, which also shows how successful delegation and empowerment can spur innovation and growth.

Parallel to this, Indra Nooyi's time as PepsiCo's CEO offers a notable illustration of empowerment and delegating. During an era of profound change, Nooyi guided PepsiCo by emphasizing sustainable growth and healthier product lines. Her capacity for effective delegation and team empowerment defined her leadership style. Seeing the value in utilizing the variety of skills that exist inside her company, Nooyi gave her senior executives significant authority.

Setting specific strategic goals and giving her team the tools and assistance they needed to reach them were key components of Nooyi's empowerment strategy. She promoted open dialogue and constructive criticism in order to create a climate of openness and cooperation. Nooyi made sure her staff was completely engaged and driven to contribute to the company's success by giving them a lot of authority. PepsiCo expanded into new product categories and markets as a result of her leadership, proving the effectiveness of empowerment in fostering strategic innovation.

In addition, empowerment and delegation are essential components of crisis management. A good example is the handling of the 1982 Tylenol issue by James Burke, the former CEO of Johnson & Johnson. Following the deaths caused by Tylenol capsules laced with cyanide, Burke faced a serious crisis that jeopardized the company's standing in the marketplace. Burke gave his staff responsibility and gave them the freedom to act quickly and decisively rather than centralizing decision-making.

Burke handled the situation by being open with his team and having faith in their expertise. He gave local managers the freedom to decide what was best for their particular surroundings and the authority to handle the problem on the ground. Johnson & Johnson was able to react swiftly and efficiently thanks to this delegation of authority, and they even made the historic choice to remove all Tylenol products from the market. Burke's crisis leadership during the crisis served as an example of how empowerment may improve organizational resilience and agility, enabling quick and efficient decisions in urgent circumstances.

Another potent illustration of empowerment and delegating in the tech sector comes from Satya Nadella's leadership at Microsoft. When Nadella took over as CEO in 2014, the business was beset by internal silos and a culture that was in decline. Nadella placed a strong emphasis on innovation and a growth mindset in his plan for Microsoft. He concentrated on empowering his staff members and building a climate of trust and cooperation in order to accomplish this.

Nadella promoted cross-functional cooperation and dismantled hierarchical obstacles as part of his empowerment strategy. He gave teams at lower organizational levels the ability to make decisions without waiting for top-down orders, enabling them to experiment and innovate. Investments in staff training and the establishment of a nurturing atmosphere where failure was viewed as a teaching opportunity helped to foster this empowerment. Microsoft underwent a culture revolution under Nadella's direction, which sparked important breakthroughs in artificial intelligence, cloud computing, and other key fields.

Giving someone authority is only one aspect of empowerment; another is giving them the tools and resources they need to succeed. This idea is demonstrated by Tony Hsieh's, the late CEO of Zappos, leadership. Hsieh was well-known for his dedication to fostering an environment at work that was empowering and upbeat. He thought that empowered and contented workers would provide great customer service, which would ultimately lead to the company's success.

Hsieh's strategy for empowerment included building an environment of trust and autonomy while decentralizing decision-making. He instituted the Holacracy management philosophy, which dispersed authority among self-organizing teams and did away with traditional managerial responsibilities. Employees were empowered by this framework to take responsibility for their work and make choices that suited their interests and strengths. Hsieh also made investments in the welfare and advancement of his staff members, offering tools for ongoing education and individual development. Through his leadership, it was shown that increased employee happiness and better organizational performance may result from empowerment.

Dr. Paul Farmer, co-founder of Partners In Health (PIH), is a remarkable example of empowerment and delegation in the nonprofit sector when it comes to global health. PIH is committed to offering the most vulnerable and impoverished communities high-quality healthcare. Farmer placed a strong emphasis on giving communities and local healthcare professionals the authority to manage their own health systems.

In order to empower and delegate, farmers partnered with neighborhood groups and trained community health professionals in healthcare delivery. He trusted the knowledge and awareness of local leaders to handle important responsibilities and to know what the demands of the community were. Farmer made ensuring that PIH's treatments were sustainable and culturally appropriate by giving local healthcare practitioners more authority. His leadership showed that in complicated and resource-constrained contexts, empowerment and delegation are essential for attaining long-term influence.

Within the field of education, Geoffrey Canada, the creator of the Harlem Children's Zone (HCZ), exemplifies how empowerment and delegation can change communities. HCZ is a comprehensive program designed to use social services, education, and community involvement to break the cycle of poverty. As a leader, Canada assigned tasks to a broad group of social workers, educators, and community organizers.

His conviction that every kid and member of the community has potential served as the foundation for Canada's empowerment strategy. He established a nurturing atmosphere that pushed team members to think creatively and customize their solutions to the particular requirements of the neighborhood. Through delegation of authority and provision of requisite resources and support, Canada enabled his team to execute comprehensive and significant programs. His leadership demonstrated the transformational power of empowerment and delegation by bringing about notable gains in community well-being and educational outcomes.

Fostering innovation and creativity also requires empowerment and delegation. Ed Catmull, co-founder of Pixar Animation Studios, offers insightful leadership on this front. Catmull placed a strong emphasis on fostering an atmosphere that encouraged creativity in his leadership style. He thought that in order to produce ground-breaking work, employees needed to be given the freedom to experiment and take chances.

As part of Catmull's empowerment strategy, decision-making was decentralized, and cooperation and open communication were encouraged. He put into practice programs like the Braintrust, which allowed filmmakers to get frank feedback from their colleagues and promote innovation and ongoing development. By giving his staff creative freedom and creating a positive work atmosphere, Catmull enabled them to push the limits of storyline and animation. His direction was crucial to Pixar's success, as the company produced a number of highly regarded and financially successful movies.

Muhammad Yunus, the creator of Grameen Bank, is a prime example of the leadership of empowerment and delegation in the context of social entrepreneurship. Grameen Bank offers microloans to underprivileged people, mostly women, so they can launch small enterprises. Under Yunus's direction, borrowers were empowered by providing them with the funds and assistance they needed to better their life.

Yunus's philosophy of empowerment was predicated on respecting and believing in the capacities of the underprivileged. He gave local employees and borrowers important duties so they could take charge of their financial decisions. Through the provision of microloans and the cultivation of a communal and supportive environment, Yunus enabled people to overcome poverty. His leadership showed how empowerment and delegation can spur social and economic development and open doors for disadvantaged groups.

Herb Kelleher, the former CEO of Southwest Airlines and co-founder, provides another powerful illustration of empowerment and delegation in the corporate world. Kelleher prioritized strong company culture and employee empowerment, which defined his leadership style. He thought that motivated staff members who were trusted and felt appreciated would provide outstanding customer service.

Kelleher's method of delegation was granting front-line staff members the power to decide in ways that improved customer satisfaction. Through his encouragement of humor, creativity, and teamwork, he created a lively and encouraging work atmosphere. Kelleher made sure Southwest Airlines maintained a high standard of customer service and operational effectiveness by giving staff members the freedom to take initiative and delegating authority. His leadership style exemplified how employee empowerment can result in a driven and enthusiastic staff, which in turn drives organizational success.

General Stanley McChrystal's leadership in the US military offers important lessons in empowerment and delegating for the public sector. Under McChrystal's direction, the Joint Special Operations Command (JSOC) was reformed to function more efficiently in a setting that was becoming more complicated and dynamic by the day. He realized that for the problems they were facing, the conventional hierarchical decision-making process was excessively stiff and sluggish.

Small, flexible teams were given more decision-making ability as part of McChrystal's empowerment strategy. He put in place a "team of teams" structure that allowed power and knowledge to move freely throughout the company. Through the delegation of authority and the enabling of team commanders to make choices on the fly, McChrystal improved the flexibility and efficiency of JSOC. Through his leadership, it was made clear that, especially in situations with high risks, empowerment is essential to improving organizational agility and responsiveness.

To sum up, effective leadership is a combination of empowerment and delegation that drives corporate success and cultivates a driven and engaged staff. There are many different methods that leaders can assign tasks and give their people more authority. Some notable examples of this are Sir Richard Branson, Indra Nooyi, James Burke, Satya Nadella, Tony Hsieh, Dr. Paul Farmer, Geoffrey Canada, Ed Catmull, Muhammad

Yunus, Herb Kelleher, and General Stanley McChrystal. These leaders have demonstrated that they can unleash the full potential of their teams, spur creativity, and produce amazing results by giving others the authority they need and giving them the support they need. Their experiences highlight the significance of recognizing and utilizing each person's special abilities, cultivating a climate of trust and cooperation, and coordinating delegation and empowerment with the strategic objectives of the company. By means of proficient delegation and empowerment, leaders may establish a dynamic and resilient organization that can flourish in a constantly evolving world.

CHAPTER 5

THE WAY OF SUCCESSFUL PEOPLE

HABITS OF HIGHLY SUCCESSFUL PEOPLE

Many times, success is attributed to a mix of skill, effort, and good fortune. But as you go deeper into the lives of really successful people, you find that these are not the only reasons behind their accomplishments. Rather, the key to their success lies in their habits, or dependable actions and routines. Their productivity, outlook, and capacity to seize life's possibilities and obstacles are all shaped by these habits. Through in-depth case studies, this chapter delves into the habits of highly successful individuals, highlighting the significant influence these routines had on their ascent to prominence.

Examine the life of one of the greatest investors of all time, Warren Buffett. Buffett's philosophy of life and business is based on a set of habits that he developed over many years. Among the most noteworthy is his dedication to lifelong learning. Buffett is renowned for reading for almost 80% of the day. He feels that information accumulates like compound interest, and the more information he has, the more knowledgeable his investing choices will be. Buffett's success has been largely attributed to his extensive reading and ongoing learning habits, which have helped him stay ahead of market trends, comprehend intricate financial processes, and make wise decisions.

Another important factor is Buffett's inclination to live a simple lifestyle. Despite his enormous riches, he leads a humble life, stays away from needless extravagance, and concentrates on the things that really count. His investment style is similarly straightforward: he looks for businesses with solid foundations and stays onto them for the long run. Buffett stays focused on his objectives and retains clarity by eschewing the diverting influences of an ostentatious lifestyle and intricate investing schemes. His behaviors highlight how crucial simplicity and ongoing learning are to attaining and maintaining success.

Comparably, Oprah Winfrey's rise from a difficult upbringing to her current status as one of the world's most powerful media moguls may be attributed to a number of behaviors that have fueled her success. A pillar of Winfrey's life has been her consistent practice of appreciation. She has always put more emphasis on what she has than what she lacks, even in the face of many obstacles. She has remained grounded because to this thankfulness practice, which has also helped her develop a positive outlook that draws possibilities and enables her to overcome obstacles with fortitude.

Winfrey also highlights her life and career's practice of intentionality. She carefully considers the initiatives she takes on, making sure they are consistent with her goals and values. Her media empire, where she utilizes her platform to encourage and uplift people, is a clear example of her intentionality. Winfrey makes deliberate and deliberate decisions to make sure her work has an impact and is meaningful, which adds to her long-term success and influence.

One other role model whose success is largely due to his habits is Steve Jobs, co-founder of Apple Inc. Jobs was renowned for his unwavering concentration. He possessed a remarkable capacity to focus on what was important and block out distractions. This emphasis played a crucial role in Apple's development of ground-breaking devices like the iPad and iPhone. By saying "no" to a thousand things in order to focus on a small number of crucial tasks, Jobs made sure that Apple could direct its resources and ingenuity on products that transformed the technology sector.

Jobs also fostered a culture of ongoing innovation. Driven by a deep-seated interest and a passion to create items that people didn't even know they needed, he consistently pushed limits and challenged the established quo. His practice of combining several domains like as technology, design, and the humanities encouraged this constant innovation habit. At Apple, Jobs made sure the business was always at the forefront of technological developments by establishing an innovative culture.

Another powerful example of how habits lead to achievement comes from the life of Harry Potter author J.K. Rowling. Rowling's persistent habit was essential to her transformation from a jobless single mother to one of the world's best-selling authors. She persisted in believing in her story and put up great effort to see it through to the end, even after receiving multiple rejections from publishers. The value of resilience and unshakable dedication to one's objectives is highlighted by this habit of endurance in the face of difficulty.

Rowling also stresses the value of having a creative and imaginative mindset. Despite facing emotional and financial difficulties, she made time each day to write and develop her creative ideas. Her ability to create the complex and engrossing universe of Harry Potter was made possible by her constant efforts to strengthen her creative abilities. Rowling's accomplishments serve as a testament to the value of tenacity and consistent practice of one's profession in producing remarkable outcomes.

Michael Jordan's illustrious basketball career serves as evidence in the realm of sports of the importance of habits in attaining success. Jordan stood out from his peers because of his unwavering practice and discipline habits. He was well-known for his intense training schedule, putting in several hours to hone his abilities and test the boundaries of his body and mind. Jordan's remarkable athleticism and competitive edge were developed by this dedicated practice routine, which helped him win six NBA titles and countless other honors.

Jordan's success was also greatly influenced by his practice of keeping an optimistic outlook. "I can accept failure, everyone fails at something," he famously remarked. However, I can't stand giving up." He was able to endure despite difficulties and setbacks because of his mentality of seeing failure as a stepping stone rather than a setback. Jordan's career serves as an example of the value of perseverance, practice, and a positive outlook in achieving the highest levels of achievement.

Facebook's COO, Sheryl Sandberg, offers yet another illuminating illustration of how habits can propel achievement, especially for women in leadership roles. Sandberg's propensity for taking chances and leaning in has helped her succeed professionally. She is an advocate for women who speak up, assume leadership positions, and confidently go after their goals. Sandberg's lean-in approach has enabled her to overcome obstacles in the male-dominated IT sector and reach noteworthy career milestones.

Additionally, Sandberg stresses the need of forming solid networks and partnerships. She frequently asks peers and mentors for assistance and offers counsel to others since she recognizes the importance of mentoring and teamwork. She has been able to create a network of allies that supports her and increases her effectiveness as a leader because to her habit of cultivating relationships. Sandberg's accomplishments highlight the value of taking calculated risks and the influence of robust professional networks.

The creator of SpaceX and Tesla, Elon Musk, is well known for his audacious ideas and inventiveness. Musk's propensity for large ideas and bold objectives has produced ground-breaking developments in renewable energy, electric cars, and space exploration. He actively strives to bring about his vision of a multiplanetary human race in the future. With his propensity for big ideas and his willingness to take chances and invest in cutting-edge technology, Musk has risen to the top of a number of businesses.

Notable is Musk's propensity for working nonstop to achieve his objectives. He is renowned for having a strong work ethic, frequently putting in long hours and being completely engrossed in the intricate intricacies of his assignments. Because of his commitment to hard work and dedication, he is able to lead his companies to achieve seemingly unattainable goals. Musk's achievement serves as a testament to the value of having a clear vision and a steadfast dedication to one's goals.

The former German Chancellor, Angela Merkel, is a prime example of the leadership trait of deliberate decision-making. Merkel is renowned for her methodical and circumspect approach to decision-making, frequently devoting time to compiling all pertinent data and taking into account all viewpoints prior to reaching a decision. Her ability to traverse complicated political environments and make judgments that have had a significant influence on Germany and the European Union is a result of her habit of careful consideration.

Merkel is particularly notable for her pragmatic and humble demeanor. She has a lot of power, yet she has always remained modest and taken a practical approach to leadership. She is respected and trusted by her peers and constituency because of her humble behavior, which has helped her govern successfully and have a lasting impact on world politics. Merkel's leadership serves as an example of how important humility and deliberate decision-making are to long-term success.

Within the field of social activism, Malala Yousafzai's narrative serves as a potent illustration of how habits influence achievement. Malala has gained international recognition as a symbol of fortitude and empowerment due to her courageous lifestyle and support of education, especially for girls. She created the Malala Fund to assist education programs globally and persisted in advocating for the right to education despite confronting potentially fatal circumstances. The campaign for educational equality has advanced significantly as a result of this courageous and activist habit, which has also inspired innumerable people worldwide.

Malala's persistence in promoting education in the face of many obstacles is another example of her habit of tenacity. She hasn't wavered from her goal of bringing about change and increasing awareness through her platform. Her accomplishment serves as a testament to the ability of bravery and tenacity to make a significant and enduring difference.

These case studies show that highly successful people's habits are based not just on their actions but also on their outlook on life and the workplace. Their success is ultimately fueled by these habits, which also mold their behavior and thinking. These habits offer a road map for attaining and maintaining success, from constant learning and simplicity to persistence, creativity, and deliberate decision-making.

It takes dedication and intentionality to form these behaviors. It entails making deliberate decisions about how to allocate your time, concentrate on certain tasks, and react to opportunities and difficulties. Successful people are aware that habits have the ability to significantly influence behavior and that they can lay the groundwork for long-term success by developing healthy habits.

Furthermore, these behaviors change and adapt throughout time; they are not set in stone. Successful people constantly improve their routines, taking lessons from past mistakes and modifying them to better suit their objectives and morals. This flexibility is essential in a world that is changing quickly and full of opportunities and new difficulties.

In short, anyone hoping to reach their objectives and leave a lasting impression can learn a lot from the practices of highly successful people. People can become more successful and resilient by forming habits like constant learning, mindfulness, intentionality, simplicity, gratitude, perseverance, and deliberate decision-making. These behaviors are essential to long-term success maintenance as well as achievement. The success of people like Malala Yousafzai, Sheryl Sandberg, Elon Musk, Oprah Winfrey, Steve Jobs, J.K. Rowling, Michael Jordan, Warren Buffett, and Sheryl Sandberg demonstrates that one's path to greatness is shaped by deliberate and consistent habits rather than just talent or luck.

TIME MANAGEMENT AND PRODUCTIVITY

Productivity and time management are essential for success in any industry. Success and productivity levels are ultimately determined by how people manage their time. This essay explores the ideas and methods of efficient time management and productivity, with examples from successful people who have mastered these techniques taken from actual case studies. We may learn a lot from their experiences on how to better manage our own time and work more efficiently.

Fundamentally, time management is planning and arranging your schedule to divide your time between several tasks. When you manage your time well, you can work more efficiently and do more tasks in less time, even under time constraints and heavy pressure. On the other side, productivity is the gauge of how well you do activities and reach objectives. These ideas collectively serve as the cornerstone of successful work practices and individual achievement.

Elon Musk, the CEO of SpaceX and Tesla, exemplifies extraordinary productivity and time management in many ways. Musk's exceptional time management abilities are demonstrated by his ability to balance several risky endeavors. Frequently putting in up to 100 hours per week, Musk is well-known for his exacting work schedule and careful time management of his multiple businesses. He uses a method known as "time blocking," where he plans his day in blocks of five minutes. With no outside distractions, this approach enables him to concentrate intently on particular tasks, resulting in optimal productivity and efficiency.

Musk's ability to rank things according to significance and urgency is evident in his calendar. He assigns his team to handle less important duties so that he can concentrate on high-impact projects that advance his companies. By using this strategy, he not only increases his output but also makes sure that his efforts are going toward things that will help him achieve his long-term objectives. Musk's achievements show how careful planning and setting priorities are essential for efficient time management and extraordinarily high levels of productivity.

The creator of Amazon, Jeff Bezos, is another noteworthy example. Bezos is renowned for using a calculated strategy when making decisions and managing his time. One of his main ideas is to make a small number of excellent decisions every day. Bezos places a high value on making critical judgments first thing in the morning because he thinks that people lose energy and their capacity for decision-making over the day. His most important decisions are made when his head is clear and his judgment is keen thanks to this habit.

Despite his busy career, Bezos also emphasizes the value of maintaining a healthy work-life balance. In order to give himself time for personal routines and creative thought, he avoids setting up meetings for early in the day. In order to sustain long-term productivity and prevent burnout, this balance is essential. Bezos' strategy shows that efficient time management involves not just working harder but also working more intelligently and taking care to maintain one's personal wellbeing.

The narrative of Steve Jobs, a co-founder of Apple Inc., is at the other extreme of the spectrum. Jobs was renowned for his extraordinary ability to concentrate on a small number of important tasks. He is credited with cutting Apple's product lineup from hundreds of things to a select few, which allowed the business to focus its resources and innovate more successfully. Jobs' time management strategy was based on the idea of simplicity. He was responsible for driving Apple's success and developing ground-breaking products by getting rid of pointless distractions and concentrating on what really important.

Jobs' dedication to concentration was also evident in his daily schedule. He was well-known for leading a simple life and having reliable routines, like wearing the same clothes every day. This lessened his decision fatigue and freed up his mind to focus more on strategic and creative thought. The success of Jobs emphasizes the value of simplicity and concentration in time management and output.

Another excellent case study in productivity and time management comes from Oprah Winfrey's career. Winfrey is a philanthropist and media magnate whose methodical time management has allowed her to amass an empire. Her ability to manage several responsibilities and endeavors is well-known; she has hosted a discussion show every day, operated her own network, and participated in charitable endeavors.

Winfrey credits her deliberate practice with a large portion of her accomplishment. She sets her priorities and aspirations for the day in meditation first thing every morning. She is better able to stay focused and coherent during the day because to this practice. In order to free up her time to concentrate on making strategic decisions and engaging in creative endeavors, Winfrey also stresses the value of assigning duties to dependable team members. Her method emphasizes the need of delegation and attention in efficient time management.

Microsoft co-founder Bill Gates provides an alternative viewpoint on productivity and time management. Gates is renowned for his meticulous time management techniques. He carefully arranges his time, setting out time for meetings, in-depth work, and leisure pursuits. In addition, Gates uses a method called "Think Weeks," in which he takes a break from his regular obligations to concentrate only on reading, reflecting, and making plans. Through this exercise, he is able to think through his objectives, acquire fresh perspectives, and plan for the future.

A further component of Gates' productivity is his dedication to lifelong learning. He reads a lot; he frequently completes a book per week. His constant learning habit keeps him energized and informed, which fuels his creativity and problem-solving skills. The accomplishments of Gates serve as an example of the value of preparation, introspection, and lifelong learning in efficient time management.

The narrative of Indra Nooyi, the former CEO of PepsiCo, sheds light on how productivity and efficient time management may propel success in the workplace. Nooyi was renowned for her methodical approach to time management and her strict work ethic. Although she frequently put in lengthy workdays, she also took sure to maintain a healthy balance between her personal and professional obligations.

Nooyi prioritized and defined definite targets in her time management strategy. She planned her day carefully to make sure she concentrated on high-impact tasks. She was incredibly organized. Additionally, Nooyi stressed the value of adaptability and resilience. She was skilled at negotiating the intricacies of an international company, acting swiftly and sensibly to lead PepsiCo toward expansion and innovation. Her accomplishments highlight how crucial goal-setting, planning, and flexibility are to efficient time management.

Serena Williams' sporting career provides insightful insights into productivity and time management. Williams, one of the all-time greats in tennis, has attained incredible success by following a strict regimen for both preparation and performance. Her daily regimen consists of mental conditioning, strategic planning, and demanding training sessions. Williams balances her training with personal obligations and professional endeavors, maintaining optimum physical and mental performance thanks to her adept time management skills.

Williams' attention to self-care and rehabilitation is another essential component of her time management. She places a high priority on her sleep, diet, and mental health since she knows that these are necessary for long-term performance and productivity. Williams' accomplishments demonstrate the value of self-care, strategic planning, and discipline in reaching and sustaining high levels of production.

The life of Facebook's COO, Sheryl Sandberg, offers an alternative viewpoint on productivity and efficient time management. Sandberg is renowned for her ability to manage both her personal and professional lives. She is an advocate of establishing limits and giving tasks priority according to their significance. Sandberg's dedication to work-life balance is demonstrated by her routine of quitting work at a respectable hour to spend time with her family.

Sandberg also stresses the significance of concentrating on work that has an impact. She pushes her staff to avoid busywork that doesn't advance the objectives of the business by identifying and prioritizing the tasks that produce the biggest outcomes. Her method shows that good time management is about matching your priorities and values with your efforts in addition to scheduling your time.

Melinda Gates's leadership in the charity sector provides insightful advice on productivity and time management. In his capacity as co-chair of the Bill & Melinda Gates Foundation, Gates oversees a wide range of programs designed to solve issues related to global health and development. Her method of managing her time consists of establishing specific goals, assigning duties, and encouraging teamwork.

Gates is renowned for her ability to pay attention to detail and maintain a broad perspective. In order to guarantee that the foundation's initiatives have an influence and are long-lasting, she sets aside time for research, strategic planning, and stakeholder engagement. The fact that Gates was able to successfully lead a complicated, multidimensional company emphasizes the value of cooperation, delegation, and strategic planning in efficient time management.

The tale of Apple Inc. CEO Tim Cook offers yet another illustration of extraordinary productivity and time management. Cook is well-known for his regimented lifestyle, which consists of frequent exercise and early mornings. He makes sure he stays aware of the requirements and experiences of Apple consumers by beginning his workday with a study of customer feedback. His leadership and decision-making style are shaped by this daily practice of putting the needs of his customers first.

Cook is also a thorough planner and setter of priorities. He plans his calendar so that he can make time for important assignments, important meetings, and his own well-being. Cook's ability to strike a balance between his work obligations and personal routines like exercise and introspection emphasizes how crucial comprehensive time management is to long-term productivity and good leadership.

Time management and productivity can be gained from historical perspectives by studying the life of Marie Curie, the pioneering scientist who conducted significant research on radioactivity. Curie had an unmatched commitment to her profession and would frequently work long hours in her laboratory. Curie overcame obstacles to become a woman in a field dominated by men, but her methodical approach to study allowed her to achieve important advances in science.

Curie's enthusiasm and dedication to her profession were the foundation of her great time management skills. She balanced her scientific endeavors with her roles as a mother and teacher by prioritizing her studies and adhering to a strict timetable. Curie's accomplishments demonstrate how a strong sense of purpose and unwavering commitment to one's objectives fuel efficient time management and productivity.

Nelson Mandela's leadership serves as yet another potent illustration of productive time management. Mandela's success was largely due to his ability to strike a balance between his personal life, leadership obligations, and political activism. Mandela made use of his time in prison to think, study, and make plans for South Africa's future. He became a resilient and astute leader due to his methodical approach to time and energy management.

Mandela's good time management is further demonstrated by his practice of placing a high priority on unity and reconciliation in his leadership. In order to make sure that his actions reflected his vision for a democratic and inclusive South Africa, he concentrated on establishing connections and encouraging communication. Mandela's leadership style exemplifies how to manage your time well by coordinating your actions with your principles and long-term objectives.

Within the field of entrepreneurship, Sara Blakely's narrative, the creator of Spanx, offers insightful insights into productivity and time management. Blakely's ability to successfully manage her time and maintain focus on her objectives is seen in her journey from selling fax machines to creating a billion-dollar company. She frequently put in a lot of overtime to balance her business endeavors with her day job.

Blakely's productivity was greatly influenced by her technique of clearly defining her objectives and picturing her accomplishment. She had an optimistic outlook and concentrated on taking concrete actions to expand her company. Blakely's accomplishment serves as a reminder of how crucial goal-setting, visualization, and persistence are to efficient time management and business success.

In conclusion, everyone looking to maximize their own performance can learn a lot from the time management and productivity habits of really successful people. The lives of Elon Musk, Jeff Bezos, Steve Jobs, Sara Blakely, Oprah Winfrey, Bill Gates, Sheryl Sandberg, Melinda Gates, Indra Nooyi, Serena Williams, Tim Cook, Marie Curie, and Nelson Mandela teach us that strategic planning, prioritization, focus, delegation, and a dedication to ongoing education and self-care are all necessary for efficient time management.

These case studies demonstrate that working smarter, not harder, is the key to success. People may increase their productivity, accomplish their goals, and keep a healthy work-life balance by using these ideas and practices. Whether you work as a scientist, corporate leader, social activist, entrepreneur, or in another field, being able to efficiently manage your time and remain productive is crucial to your long-term success and impact.

RESILIENCE AND ADAPTABILITY

Fundamental traits like resilience and adaptability help people deal with the complexity and unpredictability of life and the workplace. These qualities are especially important in the fast-paced, constantly-evolving world of today, where success or failure is determined by one's capacity to bounce back from setbacks and adapt to changing conditions. We may learn more about how resilience and adaptability support both professional and personal development by studying the lives of great people who have demonstrated these traits. This chapter examines the value of resilience and adaptation, providing in-depth case studies of accomplished individuals whose lives and careers have been influenced by these qualities.

Think about the life of Nelson Mandela, a legendary figure in the struggle against apartheid and a representation of flexibility and resiliency. Mandela faced many difficulties throughout his path, one of which was his 27-year incarceration. During this time, his fortitude was put to the test numerous times. Rather than giving in to hopelessness, Mandela made the most of his prison years by introspecting, learning, and planning for the future. He remained steadfast in his pursuit of equity and justice, showing resilience in the face of difficulty.

Mandela was also remarkably adaptable. He had to make a careful transition from revolutionary leader to statesman after being released from prison. He accepted the values of unity and reconciliation, realizing that South Africa's future depended on its ability to adjust to the new political climate. Mandela's flexibility and vision were demonstrated by his capacity for forgiveness and cooperation with his former foes. His post-apartheid leadership, which was centered on mending the nation's division, highlights the vital role that flexibility and resilience play in bringing about long-lasting change.

Malala Yousafzai, the youngest Nobel laureate, is another inspiring example. Her support of girls' education has elevated her to the status of a global symbol of adaptability and perseverance. Malala withstood a vicious attack at the age of fifteen at the hands of the Taliban, who were against her attempts to advance girls' education in Pakistan. Despite this potentially fatal event, Malala's resolve grew stronger. With even more fervor, she persisted in her activism and used her position to promote girls' rights across the globe.

Equally remarkable is Malala's capacity to adjust to her new situation following the incident. For her own safety, she moved to the UK, where she continued her activism and studies in a new setting. She was able to negotiate social and cultural divides thanks to her flexibility, and she was able to use this to change international education policy. Malala's path serves as an example of resilience, which is more than just overcoming hardship; it's also about adjusting to new circumstances and using them as a platform for constructive change.

The life narrative of former Starbucks CEO Howard Schultz provides insightful information about the value of resilience and adaptability in the workplace. Growing up in a low-income home in Brooklyn, New York, Schultz experienced several early setbacks. He was committed to succeeding in spite of these obstacles. When Schultz persuaded investors to back his plan to grow Starbucks from a small coffee bean retailer into a large chain of coffee shops throughout the world, it was clear how resilient he was.

Schultz's flexibility was essential through Starbucks' growth and several setbacks. For example, Starbucks encountered severe financial difficulties during the 2008 financial crisis. Reentering as CEO, Schultz oversaw a turnaround. He made difficult choices, such as closing failing locations and funding staff development. The business was revitalized and its growth trajectory was resumed thanks to Schultz's ability to modify his tactics in response to the shifting economic conditions. His leadership serves as an example of how resilience and adaptation are critical for overcoming obstacles in the workplace and realizing long-term success.

One of the best tennis players of all time, Serena Williams, is a prime illustration of resiliency and flexibility in action. Throughout her career, Williams has encountered several obstacles, including personal struggles and injuries. She has often proven her tenacity by rising to the top of her sport in spite of these setbacks. One of the things that has made her career so remarkable is how quickly and mentally she has been able to bounce back from losses and injuries.

Williams' ability to change up her game over time demonstrates her versatility. She modified her playing strategy as she grew older and encountered new opponents in order to stay one step ahead. She modified her tactics, welcomed new training methods, and had an open mind to development. Williams' accomplishments both on and off the court demonstrate how crucial flexibility and resilience are to reaching and maintaining greatness.

Elon Musk, the CEO of SpaceX and Tesla, is a prime example of how resilience and adaptability are critical for fostering innovation and success in the technological sector. Musk has encountered many obstacles and disappointments over his business career. Many obstacles stood in the way of his early endeavors, including Zip2 and X.com (which subsequently evolved into PayPal). But Musk's tenacity and capacity for taking lessons from these setbacks served as a springboard for his subsequent achievements.

Musk's attitude to creativity and problem-solving demonstrates his versatility. He dealt with several rocket failures at SpaceX that might have brought the firm to an end. Musk and his group didn't give up; instead, they adjusted their tactics, took lessons from their errors, and eventually accomplished successful launches. Comparably, Musk at Tesla managed to overcome obstacles related to production, finances, and fierce rivalry by constantly modifying his strategy and expanding the frontiers of electric vehicle technology. Musk's journey serves as a reminder that adaptation and resilience are essential for overcoming setbacks and realizing ground-breaking achievement.

The life narrative of Oprah Winfrey also offers a powerful example of flexibility and perseverance. Winfrey overcome a difficult upbringing filled with abuse and poverty to rise to prominence as one of the world's most powerful media moguls. Her will to succeed in spite of these early setbacks demonstrated her tenacity. Winfrey's ascent to fame was propelled by her capacity to relate to people and share her experiences in a real way with audiences.

Winfrey's capacity to adapt was crucial to the development of her profession. She hosted a nationally syndicated talk show after making a seamless transition from local journalism, changing both her tone and subject matter to appeal to a wider audience. As she started her own television network and branched out into other commercial endeavors, Winfrey demonstrated her capacity to continuously reinvent herself. Her accomplishments show how resilient and adaptable one must be to take advantage of new chances and maintain long-term success in a changing business.

The life of Harry Potter series author J.K. Rowling serves as additional evidence of the value of resilience and flexibility. Prior to becoming a well-known author, Rowling had to overcome numerous obstacles in her personal and professional life, such as being a welfare-dependent single mother. She persevered through these difficulties and committed herself to writing and editing her manuscript.

Rowling's ability to adjust was essential after her book was turned down by several publishers. She persisted in looking for chances and eventually got a publishing deal rather than giving up. The popularity of the Harry Potter books presented her with new difficulties, such as juggling celebrity and pursuing more creative endeavors. The secret to Rowling's ongoing success has been her ability to adjust to these changes without sacrificing her originality or creative vision. Her story demonstrates the importance of resilience and adaptability in overcoming early obstacles and navigating the complexity of success.

The scientific community may learn a great deal from Marie Curie's life about resiliency and flexibility. Even though Curie was a woman working in an area that was predominately male, she overcame several obstacles to continue her scientific studies. Her unwavering work ethic and determination in the face of scarce resources and acknowledgment demonstrated her resilience.

Curie's versatility played a pivotal role in her seminal findings on radioactivity. She worked with other scientists, modified her research techniques, and overcame the difficulties of handling hazardous materials. Two Nobel Prizes and important scientific breakthroughs were the result of her inventiveness and capacity to modify her strategy. Curie's tale serves as an example of how flexibility and resilience are crucial for expanding the frontiers of knowledge and producing scientific discoveries.

The life narrative of Facebook's COO, Sheryl Sandberg, sheds light on the value of flexibility and resilience in leadership. Throughout his career, Sandberg has experienced both personal tragedy and professional triumph. When she experienced the unexpected death of her husband, Dave Goldberg, her fortitude was put to the test. Despite the severe effects of this loss, Sandberg showed resiliency by candidly discussing her experience with bereavement and healing, encouraging others going through a similar ordeal.

Sandberg's leadership style at Facebook demonstrates her flexibility. She managed the intricacies of a quickly expanding tech business, modifying her tactics to take advantage of fresh chances and obstacles. Many women have been given the courage to take leadership roles and confidently navigate their jobs because to Sandberg's emphasis on leaning in and taking chances. Her experience serves as a reminder of how important flexibility and resilience are to both effective leadership and personal development.

Steve Jobs, a co-founder of Apple Inc., has a business career that emphasizes the value of perseverance and adaptation. Among the many obstacles Jobs had to overcome was being fired from Apple, the firm he co-founded. He showed resiliency in the face of this severe setback by starting NeXT and making investments in Pixar, both of which prospered. When Jobs returned to Apple and oversaw its metamorphosis into one of the most valuable companies in the world, his ability to take what he had learned from these events and modify his techniques was essential.

Jobs' flexibility was shown in the way he approached innovation and product development. He consistently pushed the limits of technology and design, making adjustments to reflect shifting customer tastes and industry trends. Jobs changed several sectors with his attention on user experience, visual design, and simplicity. His experience serves as a reminder that, in a highly competitive setting, innovation must be driven by perseverance and adaptation in order to achieve long-term success.

The biography of Germany's former chancellor, Angela Merkel, offers a political viewpoint on flexibility and endurance. Throughout her term, Merkel had to deal with a number of difficulties, such as managing the world financial crisis, the European refugee crisis, and changing political environments. Her steadfast leadership and capacity to keep things stable in the face of turbulence were clear indicators of her resilience.

Merkel's flexibility was essential to her approach to foreign relations and policymaking. She modified her tactics to deal with complicated and changing problems by striking a balance between her dedication to her basic ideals and practical decision-making. Merkel's leadership in maintaining European unity and handling crises highlights the significance of flexibility and resilience in political leadership.

Within the field of social activity, Mahatma Gandhi's life offers a compelling illustration of flexibility and perseverance. Gandhi had to contend with a great deal of opposition and hardship in his struggle to free India from British domination. His steadfast dedication to nonviolent resistance in the face of several incarcerations and violent retaliation demonstrated his resilience.

Gandhi led the Indian independence struggle with remarkable flexibility. In order to meet shifting political realities and rally a variety of groups, he modified his tactics. Gandhi's emphasis on independence, civil disobedience, and nonviolent protest struck a chord around the world and sparked more social justice movements. His life serves as an example of how flexibility and resilience are necessary to promote social change and accomplish group objectives.

Within the corporate realm, Mary Barra, the CEO of General Motors, offers valuable perspectives on the significance of resilience and adaptation. When Barra took over as CEO of GM, she had to deal with a number of difficult issues, such as the aftermath of a large-scale vehicle recall and the company's transition within the quickly changing automotive sector. Her ability to steer the business through these problems and enact big reforms demonstrated her resilience.

Barra's flexibility was essential to her approach to leadership and innovation. She led GM's transition to electric and driverless vehicles, modifying the business's tactics to meet new market needs and trends. Barra's emphasis on creating an environment of transparency and accountability has been crucial to GM's comeback. Her leadership serves as an example of how resilience and adaptation are critical for bringing about long-term success inside a company.

In conclusion, it is impossible to overestimate the value of adaptation and resilience. We can see that these traits are necessary for overcoming hardship, navigating change, and achieving long-term success through the lives and careers of Nelson Mandela, Malala Yousafzai,

Howard Schultz, Serena Williams, Elon Musk, Oprah Winfrey, J.K. Rowling, Marie Curie, Sheryl Sandberg, Steve Jobs, Angela Merkel, Mahatma Gandhi, and Mary Barra. While flexibility enables people to change their tactics and seize new chances, resilience enables people to bounce back from setbacks and stay focused on their objectives. When combined, these qualities provide the groundwork for both professional and personal development, enabling people to prosper in a world that is constantly evolving.

CONTINUES LEARNING AND IMPROVEMENT

Personal and professional growth are propelled by the fundamental concepts of continuous learning and improvement. These ideas entail a dedication to ongoing self-reflection, flexibility, and the quest of new information and abilities. The capacity to continuously learn and grow is necessary in a world where change is constant if one wants to succeed, remain relevant, and make significant contributions. This chapter explores the value of ongoing education and development, with real-world case studies of people who have demonstrated these ideas in both their personal and professional lives.

Take the life of Bill Gates, one of the most prosperous businessmen in the world and a co-founder of Microsoft, for example. Gates' path serves as a reminder of the value of ongoing education and development. Gates showed a ravenous hunger for knowledge from a young age. He studied extensively and gained knowledge on a wide range of topics, setting the groundwork for his future achievements. He remained dedicated to learning throughout his professional life.

Gates promoted innovation and a culture of constant improvement at Microsoft. He supported his team's efforts to grow from both setbacks and victories, believing in the transformative potential of feedback. Microsoft was able to keep its competitive edge and adjust to shifting technological trends because to this strategy. Even after leaving his daily position at Microsoft, Bill Gates made education his top priority. He has taken on challenging global issues through the Bill and Melinda Gates Foundation, always looking for fresh insights and solutions. The narrative of Bill Gates demonstrates the necessity of ongoing education and development in order to maintain success and leave a lasting impression.

Within the sports domain, the career of the late basketball legend Kobe Bryant offers a striking illustration of ongoing education and development. Bryant has an unmatched commitment to his craft. He was well-known for his unwavering work ethic and his constant search for methods to enhance his abilities and output. He painstakingly examined game tape, took lessons from his errors, and modified his training regimens to improve his performance.

Beyond basketball, Bryant was a lifelong student. He studied a variety of subjects, including business and storytelling, and was an enthusiastic reader. Following his retirement from the NBA, Bryant used his growth attitude to pursue new endeavors in writing and production. His Academy Award-winning animated short film, "Dear Basketball," proved he could be successful in an entirely other industry. Bryant's life serves as an example of how success and achievement in a variety of fields may result from ongoing learning and development.

The biography of Marie Curie provides a historical viewpoint on lifelong learning and scientific advancement. Even though Curie was a woman working in an area that was predominately male, she overcame several obstacles to continue her scientific studies. Her unwavering quest for knowledge produced ground-breaking radioactive discoveries. Curie's unwavering work ethic and openness to trying out novel concepts and approaches demonstrated her dedication to lifelong learning.

Curie had a comprehensive approach to education. She worked with other scientists, kept up with the most recent findings, and modified her methods to get around challenges. Her two Nobel Prizes in separate scientific domains for her discoveries are evidence of her never-ending learning curve. Curie's tale serves as a reminder that expanding one's knowledge and making scientific discoveries require a dedication to study and flexibility.

The inventor of Spanx, Sara Blakely, demonstrates via her entrepreneurial career the value of ongoing education and development in the business world. Although Blakely's career began with marketing fax machines, she had a concept for a novel kind of underwear for ladies. Blakely depended on her inventiveness and eagerness to learn because she had no formal background in business or fashion. To improve her product, she investigated the market, looked into the materials, and asked for input.

Blakely's approach to creating Spanx demonstrated her dedication to ongoing development. She modified her designs based on input from customers and kept coming up with new ideas to satisfy their demands. Her tenacity and growth-oriented mentality made Spanx a billion-dollar company. Blakely's tale demonstrates the importance of ongoing education and development for both entrepreneurship and producing consumer-pleasing goods.

In the business sector, Satya Nadella, the CEO of Microsoft, is a prime example of how organizational transformation is impacted by ongoing learning and development. Microsoft faced many difficulties when Nadella took over, including internal stagnation and a decline in market relevance. Nadella gave learning a high priority at all organizational levels and adopted a growth attitude.

Microsoft adopted a continuous improvement culture and turned its attention to cloud computing under Nadella's direction. He pushed staff members to experiment with new concepts, work across teams, and learn from mistakes. This change in culture brought Microsoft back to life and spurred substantial expansion and innovation. The tale of Nadella shows that maintaining competitiveness in a market that is changing quickly requires constant learning and development within a company.

The media mogul and philanthropist Oprah Winfrey's career offers yet another compelling illustration of lifelong learning and development. Winfrey's path from a difficult upbringing to her status as one of the media industry's most powerful personalities is typified by her dedication to both personal and professional development. Throughout her career, Winfrey never stopped learning and growing in order to improve her abilities and reach a wider audience.

Winfrey took a comprehensive approach to education. She read widely, conversed with influential people, and incorporated fresh perspectives into her writing. Her capacity for growth and adaptation helped "The Oprah Winfrey Show" and her other business endeavors endure. Winfrey's dedication to education permeated her charitable endeavors as well, as she looked for creative answers to pressing social problems. Her experience serves as a reminder that making significant progress and attaining long-term success require constant learning.

Elon Musk, the CEO of SpaceX and Tesla, is a prime example of how innovation in the technology sector is fueled by ongoing learning and development. Musk's quest is distinguished by his boundless curiosity and eagerness to take on daring tasks. He never stops learning new things and using them to tackle challenging issues in renewable energy, electric cars, and space exploration.

Musk's practical approach to his endeavors demonstrates his dedication to learning. To make his goods better, he works with experts, gets lost in technical minutiae, and refines his designs again. Tesla has led the electric vehicle revolution and SpaceX has accomplished significant milestones in space flight because to this learning attitude. Musk's narrative highlights the need of ongoing learning and development in order to push the frontiers of invention and achieve game-changing success.

The career of former PepsiCo CEO Indra Nooyi offers insights into the significance of ongoing education and development for business leadership. Nooyi's strategic vision and dedication to sustainability defined her time at PepsiCo. In order to direct the expansion of the business and tackle new issues, she was always looking for fresh information and perspectives.

Nooyi studied industry trends, welcomed new technologies, and listened to a variety of viewpoints when learning. She put policies into place to encourage healthier products and lessen their negative effects on the environment, modifying PepsiCo's tactics to suit shifting consumer tastes. Nooyi's leadership exemplifies how long-term value creation and sustainable growth depend on ongoing learning and development.

One of the most successful directors in history, Steven Spielberg, has a career in entertainment that serves as a testament to the value of lifelong learning and personal growth in artistic endeavors. Spielberg's continuing success can be largely attributed to his ability to adjust to new technologies and storytelling approaches. He makes an ongoing effort to learn new things and try out novel concepts to make sure that his work is effective and current.

Spielberg's varied body of work, which covers a wide range of genres and issues, demonstrates his dedication to ongoing progress. He works with creative people, follows business developments, and adopts new filmmaking technologies. Spielberg's narrative serves as an example of how maintaining creativity and attaining artistic greatness require constant learning and development.

The founder of Alibaba Group, Jack Ma, demonstrates through his entrepreneurial path the importance of ongoing learning and development in creating a worldwide enterprise. Ma's road to prosperity was not an easy one. It took him many rejections and disappointments before he founded Alibaba. His dedication to acquiring new skills and adjusting remained constant, though.

Ma never stopped looking for fresh perspectives and information to direct Alibaba's expansion. He researched international markets, took notes from other prosperous companies, and pushed his group to be creative. Alibaba became a market leader in e-commerce and technology because to this learning mentality. Ma's tale shows that overcoming obstacles and succeeding as an entrepreneur require constant learning and development.

The literary career of Harry Potter series creator J.K. Rowling offers a powerful illustration of lifelong learning and development. Before becoming a well-known author, Rowling had to overcome severe financial and personal hardships. Her journey was significantly influenced by her tenacity and dedication to education.

Rowling constantly improved her writing, made edits to her drafts, and took criticism to heart. The extraordinary success of the Harry Potter series was largely attributed to her ability to modify her storytelling to engage readers. Rowling showed her dedication to constant growth by continuing to write and experiment with different genres even after her breakthrough. Her experience demonstrates that attaining and maintaining artistic achievement requires a commitment to learning and development.

Mahatma Gandhi's life provides an insightful viewpoint on lifelong learning and development within the framework of social engagement. Gandhi's dedication to social justice and nonviolent resistance characterized his life's work. He was always on the lookout for fresh information and perspectives to improve his tactics and accomplish his objectives.

Gandhi studied a wide range of ideas, interacted with a wide range of cultures, and modified his teaching strategies in response to shifting conditions. His capacity to pick up new skills and refine his strategy was essential to organizing a large-scale movement and winning India's independence. Gandhi's narrative serves as an example of how constant learning and development are necessary to promote social change and accomplish group objectives.

Business-wise, Jeff Bezos, the creator of Amazon, is a prime example of how successful entrepreneurship is impacted by ongoing learning and development. Bezos's unwavering quest of innovation and client delight has defined his career. He is always looking for fresh perspectives and information to help steer Amazon's development.

Bezos's willingness to take risks and experimentation demonstrates his dedication to learning. He promotes a continuous improvement culture at Amazon, giving staff members the freedom to experiment and grow from mistakes. Amazon's ability to adopt a learning attitude has allowed it to rise to the top of several industries, including cloud computing and e-commerce. The life narrative of Bezos shows how innovation and long-term success depend on ongoing learning and development.

The life and work of international champion of girls' education Malala Yousafzai sheds light on the importance of lifelong learning and development in social engagement. Malala's journey is distinguished by her steadfast dedication to empowerment and education. She overcame obstacles that could have killed her, but she persisted in going to school and speaking up for other people.

Malala's method of learning is keeping up with world events, working with different stakeholders, and modifying her advocacy tactics to get the most impact. Her capacity to adapt and refine her methods has increased her impact and voice, making a substantial global contribution to the advancement of girls' education. Malala's tale serves as a reminder that societal change and long-lasting effects require constant learning and development.

To sum up, the core ideas that propel both professional and personal progress are ongoing learning and development. These principles are necessary for attaining greatness and contributing significantly, as demonstrated by the life case studies of Bill Gates, Kobe Bryant, Marie Curie, Sara Blakely, Satya Nadella, Oprah

Winfrey, Elon Musk, Indra Nooyi, Steven Spielberg, Jack Ma, J.K. Rowling, Mahatma Gandhi, Jeff Bezos, and Malala Yousafzai. While continuous development necessitates the willingness to modify and enhance one's approach, continual learning entails a dedication to searching out new information and insights. When combined, these attributes serve as the cornerstone of success, allowing people to prosper in a world that is always changing and make a lasting impression.

CHAPTER 6

BUILDING A STRONG TEAM

RECRUITING THE RIGHT PEOPLE

The success of any organization depends on hiring the appropriate people, which is both an art and a science. An organization's performance, creativity, and growth can be greatly impacted by its capacity to find, draw in, and hold onto talent that is compatible with its objectives and culture. This chapter explores the nuances of successful hiring, highlighting the significance of this process using a variety of real-world case studies of successful hiring executives and businesses.

Take Google, for instance, which is well-known for its inventive and stringent hiring procedures. The goal of Google's hiring process is to find candidates who share the company's values of innovation, teamwork, and constant progress in addition to having outstanding skill sets. To examine applicants thoroughly, the organization uses a mix of behavioral evaluations, problem-solving exercises, and structured interviews.

Google's dominance in the tech industry and its constant position as one of the greatest places to work are testaments to its effectiveness in hiring the right individuals. Innovation is encouraged by the company's emphasis on selecting people who have a strong potential for learning and development. Google's dedication to diversity and inclusivity in its hiring practices contributes to its capacity to draw in a diverse pool of talent and fosters innovation and multifaceted problem-solving.

Southwest Airlines is an intriguing case study as well, as the airline has based its success on a distinctive and successful recruitment strategy. As attitudes and personalities are innate, abilities can be taught, but cultural fit is highly valued at Southwest Airlines. The hiring process at the organization places a strong emphasis on finding applicants who share its fundamental values of positivity, teamwork, and customer service.

Multiple interview rounds are a part of Southwest's recruitment process, and group interviews are frequently used to watch candidates' relationships with one another. This approach assists the business in finding people who are motivated, competent, and compatible with the customer-focused culture of the airline. Southwest's reputation for providing exceptional customer service and its continuously high staff satisfaction levels are testaments to the effectiveness of this strategy.

The tale of online shoe and apparel store Zappos provides insights into creative hiring techniques in the retail industry. The unique corporate culture of Zappos is well-known for emphasizing enjoyment, originality, and customer service. The goal of the company's hiring procedure is to find candidates that perfectly match the company's culture in addition to being highly skilled.

A distinctive two-part interview method is used by Zappos; the first portion evaluates experience and qualifications, while the second part considers cultural fit. Questions about the candidates' personalities, ideals, and approaches to different situations are posed. Furthermore, if a new hire decides after the first week that they are not a good fit for the company, they can leave with a $2,000 incentive from Zappos. By using this tactic, Zappos can be sure that individuals who choose to stay are sincere believers in the company's values. Zappos has a successful strategy, as seen by the high levels of consumer loyalty and employee engagement.

Apple's hiring practices under Steve Jobs offer another intriguing example in the IT sector. Jobs felt that employing A-players with passion and ambition in addition to talent was important. He frequently took an active role in the hiring process, making sure that potential new hires adhered to his exacting standards.

Apple has a rigorous hiring procedure that included several rounds of interviews and hands-on training. Jobs sought out people who could question the existing quo and support Apple's innovative culture. Because of its careful hiring practices, Apple was able to assemble a group of incredibly gifted people who were instrumental in creating ground-breaking products and propelling the business's growth. The innovative history and market supremacy of Apple are testaments to Jobs' emphasis on hiring the best candidates.

Goldman Sachs' hiring procedures in the finance industry provide insight into how crucial it is to find the appropriate people. Goldman Sachs is renowned for its stringent hiring procedures, which involve case studies, aptitude testing, and many interview rounds. The company is looking for people who have excellent analytical and interpersonal abilities in addition to their technical ability.

At Goldman Sachs, cultural fit is highly valued. The company seeks applicants who share its commitment to excellence, teamwork, and honesty. The goal of the company's hiring procedure is to find candidates who can succeed in a fast-paced, high-pressure work environment and add to its long-term success. Because of its emphasis on selecting qualified candidates, Goldman Sachs has been able to uphold its standing as one of the top investment banks with a bright and committed staff.

One of the most successful football teams in the world, FC Barcelona, offers insights into the value of talent development and identification through their recruitment tactics. La Masia, FC Barcelona's esteemed development program, is dedicated to spotting young talent and developing their abilities from an early age. The squad seeks players that share its devotion, collaboration, humility, and style of play in addition to their technical skill.

During the recruitment process at La Masia, young players from all around the world are scouted, and their potential is evaluated through training sessions and trials. The academy offers a comprehensive development program that covers instruction, technical training, and individual growth. A number of elite players, such as Lionel Messi, Xavi Hernandez, and Andres Iniesta, have come out of La Masia, demonstrating the effectiveness of FC Barcelona's recruitment approach. These players have made a substantial contribution to the team's many triumphs and stellar reputation for elegant, technical football.

Within the hotel sector, Ritz-Carlton's hiring procedures are considered industry benchmarks for superior customer service. Those with a passion for providing outstanding customer experiences and a natural flair for hospitality are the ones that Ritz-Carlton seeks out for employment. The organization seeks applicants with a strong service orientation, sensitivity, and attention to detail.

Behavioral interviews, role-playing exercises, and evaluations of candidates' compliance with the Gold Standards of service set forth by the corporation are all part of Ritz-Carlton's hiring process. To make sure they understand and uphold the company's dedication to quality, new personnel go through a rigorous training program. The success of Ritz-Carlton's hiring and training initiatives is demonstrated by the hotel chain's devoted clientele and multiple accolades for customer service.

Teach For America (TFA), a non-profit organization, provides an illustration of successful hiring procedures meant to tackle social issues. The goal of TFA is to end educational inequality by finding and training exceptional teachers to work in underprivileged areas. The goal of the organization's hiring procedure is to find applicants who are not just highly qualified academically but also fervently dedicated to social justice and educational change.

A tough application, interviews, and a practice teaching session are all part of TFA's selection process. The group seeks out people who have a strong desire to make a difference, perseverance, and leadership potential. TFA candidates go through rigorous training after being chosen, preparing them for the difficulties of working as teachers in high-need schools. The beneficial effects that TFA's teachers have on students' academic performance and the long-term contributions that many of its graduates make to education and social policy demonstrate the effectiveness of the organization's recruitment strategy.

Toyota's hiring procedures in the auto industry provide valuable insights into the significance of matching talent with the objectives and values of the firm. Toyota places a strong emphasis on respect for people and continual development (Kaizen) in addition to technical skills when employing new employees. The organization is looking for people that share its commitment to quality, innovation, and teamwork.

Toyota uses a multi-phase interviewing process in addition to aptitude tests and practical evaluations in their hiring process. The organization also looks closely at cultural fit, seeking applicants who can flourish in its culture of teamwork and process-driven work. Toyota's success in the worldwide auto industry and its reputation for quality and innovation are testaments to the efficacy of its hiring procedures.

Within the academic sphere, eminent universities like Harvard's hiring procedures offer insight into the significance of choosing the best candidates for outstanding instruction. The goal of Harvard's extremely tough admissions process is to find applicants who possess extraordinary academic ability, the potential to be leaders, and a dedication to changing the world.

A comprehensive examination of candidates' academic records, standardized test results, personal essays, and extracurricular involvement are all part of the admissions process. Harvard looks for students who are varied in their backgrounds and viewpoints in addition to being intellectually interested. The accomplishments of Harvard's alumni, who go on to make important contributions in a variety of professions, and the university's continuously high academic standards attest to the effectiveness of its recruitment strategy.

The recruiting processes of Internet startups such as Airbnb underscore the significance of selecting the proper personnel in order to foster innovation and expansion. The founders of Airbnb placed a high value on cultural fit and alignment with the company's goal of fostering a feeling of community. Multiple interviews, real-world assignments, and evaluations of candidates' capacity to contribute to a dynamic, cooperative work environment are all part of the company's hiring procedure.

A major contributor to Airbnb's quick development and success has been its dedication to selecting people who share its vision and core principles. The company has revolutionized the travel and hotel sector by its ability to draw in and hold on to elite personnel, which has allowed it to consistently develop and extend its products.

In conclusion, any organization's ability to attract and hire qualified candidates is essential to its success. Employing a combination of identifying technical skills, evaluating cultural fit, and matching candidates with organizational values and goals are the components of effective recruitment practices, as demonstrated by the real-world case studies of Google, Southwest Airlines, Zappos, Apple, Goldman Sachs, FC Barcelona, Ritz-Carlton, Teach For America, Toyota, Harvard, and Airbnb. These illustrations show how a systematic approach to hiring may stimulate creativity, improve output, and support sustained success. Organizations must constantly learn and adjust their recruitment procedures if they want to be competitive and accomplish their goals in a world that is changing quickly.

FOSTERING A POSITIVE TEAM CULTURE

In any firm, building a positive team culture is critical to success. Collaboration, engagement, and productivity are all boosted by a positive team culture, which directs the group's efforts toward common objectives. This chapter explores the complexities of developing and maintaining a positive team culture, using real-world case studies of successful leaders and companies to highlight key points.

The Google tale is among the most powerful illustrations of cultivating a positive team culture. Since its founding, Google has made a big deal out of fostering an environment at work where staff members feel inspired, empowered, and respected. Larry Page and Sergey Brin, the company's founders, thought that performance and innovation would be spurred by an upbeat and welcoming atmosphere. They put into effect procedures that promoted candid conversation, imagination, and a feeling of community.

Employees at Google are urged to think creatively and take chances. Employees are permitted to devote 20% of their workday to initiatives they are enthusiastic about, even if they have nothing to do with their official duties, thanks to the company's well-known "20% time" policy.

Some of Google's most successful products, such Gmail and Google News, are the result of this philosophy. Google has created an atmosphere where workers are inspired to provide their best work by valuing creativity and independence.

Google's strong team culture also includes a strong emphasis on open communication and openness. Regular "TGIF" meetings are held by the corporation where staff members can ask senior management, including the CEO, direct questions. Because they believe their thoughts are valued and their voices are heard, employees are more likely to feel trusted and included as a result of this approach. Google's emphasis on openness and communication has played a significant role in creating a supportive and cooperative work environment.

Ritz-Carlton is well-known in the hospitality sector for its superb customer service and encouraging work environment. With "We are Ladies and Gentlemen serving Ladies and Gentlemen," as its motto, the business pledges to treat both clients and staff with dignity and respect. Ritz-Carlton's methodical hiring procedure, which emphasizes selecting people who share the company's values and service philosophy, is the first step in creating a healthy team culture.

Employees go through a rigorous training program after being hired to make sure they comprehend and uphold Ritz-Carlton's high standards of excellence. The business makes significant investments in the professional growth of its staff members by providing ongoing training and chances for promotion. Additionally, Ritz-Carlton gives its staff members the freedom to decide how best to improve the guest experience by allowing them to handle problems and go above and beyond for guests.

The company's "Gold Standards" of service, which offer a precise structure for workers to adhere to while simultaneously permitting flexibility and individual initiative, enable this empowerment. Ritz-Carlton has established a work environment where employees are inspired to provide great service and take pride in their profession by cultivating a culture of empowerment and trust. The end effect is a highly engaged workforce that adds to the company's stellar reputation and devoted clientele.

Netflix is an intriguing case study in the technology industry for cultivating a positive team culture because of its innovative approach to employee flexibility and corporate governance. The core values of Netflix's culture are "Freedom and Responsibility." The organization thinks it can draw in and keep top talent if it gives workers autonomy over decisions and accountability for achieving goals.

In Netflix's culture, open communication, honest criticism, and lifelong learning are valued. Employees are encouraged to communicate honestly and openly, and they are expected to regularly provide and receive constructive criticism. This technique encourages a culture of accountability and excellent performance in addition to personal growth and development.

Additionally, Netflix gives its workers a great deal of discretion over how they handle their jobs. Employees are trusted to manage their time and produce outcomes; there are no tight vacation regulations or set working hours. This high degree of trust and adaptability fosters a positive and inspiring work environment by enabling individuals to take responsibility for their job. Netflix's ability to develop quickly and innovate in the fiercely competitive entertainment sector can be attributed in large part to its efforts to cultivate a healthy work culture.

Within the retail industry, the Costco narrative sheds light on how crucial employee loyalty and happiness are to building a positive team environment. Costco is renowned for offering competitive pay and benefits, like as retirement plans, full health insurance, and competitive wages. The business thinks it can guarantee excellent customer service and operational efficiency by looking after its staff.

In addition to offering plenty of options for career progression, Costco promotes employees from within in an effort to promote a healthy team culture. The business makes investments in the training and development of its employees, enabling them to grow in the firm and gain new skills. This emphasis on the loyalty and development of employees has produced a highly motivated and engaged staff with minimal employee turnover and excellent job satisfaction levels.

The knowledgable, amiable, and dedicated staff at Costco are a testament to the company's healthy team culture and their commitment to giving customers an excellent shopping experience. The company's excellent financial performance and standing as a top retailer are partly attributable to its achievement in building a positive work culture.

Within the realm of athletics, the New Zealand All Blacks rugby team provides a striking illustration of how to cultivate a healthy team culture via leadership and principles. One of the greatest sports teams in history, the All Blacks are renowned for both their strong team spirit and their on-field accomplishments.

The fundamental principles of the All Blacks' culture are respect, humility, and never-ending improvement. Players are raised with these ideals from an early age and have them reinforced throughout their careers. Members of the team are required to maintain the greatest standards of behavior both on and off the field, and they are emphasized to prioritize the good of the team over personal interests.

Building a positive team culture within the All Blacks is mostly dependent on leadership. Senior athletes and coaches set an exemplary example by being disciplined, committed, and unrelenting in their pursuit of perfection. This kind of leadership creates a team environment where everyone is driven to contribute to the success of the group and feels a feeling of unity and purpose.

The All Blacks also put a lot of focus on ongoing education and development. To find areas for improvement, the team solicits feedback and evaluates performance on a regular basis. The All Blacks have been able to preserve their winning team culture and domination in international rugby because to their dedication to excellence and constant progress.

The business narrative of outdoor apparel and equipment manufacturer Patagonia emphasizes the significance of integrating social and environmental principles into corporate culture. Patagonia's dedication to social responsibility and environmental sustainability is ingrained in the company's culture. "We're in business to save our home planet," the company's mission statement, embodies its commitment to these principles.

By encouraging staff members to take part in environmental action and giving them chances to have a positive influence, Patagonia promotes a positive team culture. The corporation promotes programs that encourage sustainability and conservation and provides paid time off for employees to volunteer for environmental causes. When a company's practices and mission connect, it gives its employees a sense of purpose and fulfillment.

Positive team culture at Patagonia is further enhanced by the company's dedication to ethical and transparent business methods. The business strives to maintain sustainable environmental practices and fair labor conditions, and it is transparent about its supplier chain policies. Patagonia has created an incredibly devoted and enthusiastic staff that is committed to the company's goals and values by cultivating a culture of honesty and accountability.

The way that Mayo Clinic cultivates a positive team culture offers important insights for the healthcare industry. Mayo Clinic is well known for its collaborative approach to healthcare delivery and patient-centered care. The culture of the company places a strong emphasis on respect, cooperation, and ongoing education.

The guiding principle of Mayo Clinic's good team culture is "the needs of the patient come first." In order to deliver the best treatment possible, healthcare professionals collaborate in an environment that is fostered by this guiding philosophy. The company promotes interdisciplinary teamwork and open communication to make sure that each team member's area of specialty is recognized and used.

Mayo Clinic also makes investments in the training and welfare of its staff. The company provides extensive training programs, chances for career advancement, and assistance with work-life balance. By placing a high priority on the growth and well-being of its employees, Mayo Clinic creates a happy and encouraging work atmosphere that improves both patient care and employee satisfaction.

The way Finland's educational system promotes a positive team culture provides insightful information for the education sector. Finland is renowned for having an excellent educational system that places a strong emphasis on fairness, cooperation, and the welfare of the students. Finnish schools encourage cooperation between educators, learners, and parents in order to create a positive team culture.

In Finland, educators are accorded great respect and considerable latitude in their professional endeavors. Teachers are encouraged to work together, exchange best practices, and keep refining their instructional strategies. A flat organizational structure that values equal collaboration between teachers and school administrators supports this collaborative culture.

The entire development and well-being of students are given top priority in Finnish schools. The goal of the educational system is to give kids access to a safe, accepting, and stimulating environment where they can explore their interests and abilities. By placing a strong focus on wellbeing and teamwork, schools can foster a pleasant culture that improves learning results and student engagement.

Within the domain of technology startups, Slack's culture is an intriguing illustration of cultivating a positive team culture via openness, inclusivity, and ongoing enhancement. The success of the collaboration tool Slack has been based on a welcoming and upbeat workplace culture that emphasizes candid communication and worker autonomy.

The culture of Slack is known for its high degree of transparency, as staff members are regularly updated on corporate decisions and developments. The business encourages team members to work together and communicate freely by using its own platform. Among the staff, this openness promotes trust and a feeling of community.

Another important element of Slack's positive team culture is diversity and inclusion. The organization is dedicated to fostering an inclusive workplace where each worker is treated with respect and feels appreciated. Comprehensive training programs, employee resource groups, and campaigns to guarantee fair hiring procedures are just a few of Slack's endeavors to support diversity and inclusion.

Another pillar of Slack's culture is continuous improvement. Employees are encouraged to ask for criticism, try out novel concepts, and gain knowledge from their experiences. Slack's emphasis on ongoing education and development keeps it creative and adaptable to its users' requirements.

In conclusion, each organization's potential to succeed and last depends on cultivating a positive team culture. Transparency, inclusion, empowerment, and continuous development are the cornerstones of a strong team culture, as demonstrated by the following real-world case studies: Google, Ritz-Carlton, Netflix, Costco, the New Zealand All Blacks, Patagonia, Mayo Clinic, Finland's educational system, and Slack. These illustrations show how creating a positive team culture strategically may boost creativity, improve output, and lead to long-term success. Through fostering an atmosphere that makes workers feel appreciated, inspired, and involved in the company's goals, leaders can develop a productive and upbeat team culture that promotes both individual and group development.

EFFECTIVE TEAM COMMUNICATION

A key component of any successful organization is efficient team communication. Collaboration, problem-solving, and invention all depend on one's capacity to communicate ideas effectively, listen intently, and promote candid communication. This chapter examines the components of successful team communication and provides real-world case studies of businesses that have mastered this important teamwork skill.

The Pixar Animation Studios is widely recognized for its exceptional teamwork in communicating. Pixar's astonishing communication culture, in addition to its technological prowess, is the reason behind its success in producing blockbuster animated pictures. Pixar co-founder Ed Catmull highlighted the value of a transparent and honest work atmosphere where all staff members feel comfortable offering suggestions and criticism.

Pixar's "Braintrust" gatherings serve as evidence of this methodology. These are gatherings where directors show their work to a group of seasoned filmmakers in order to discuss the status of ongoing projects. The criticism is direct and helpful, concentrating on how to enhance the narrative without compromising the director's intentions. These sessions work best when they are held in a non-hierarchical setting where everyone can participate in the conversation, regardless of status. Creativity and problem-solving are encouraged in this environment of open communication, which has been essential to Pixar's continuous success.

Within the tech sector, Amazon serves as an example of how communication is critical to fostering creativity and efficiency. The creator of Amazon, Jeff Bezos, established a communication style that promotes direct, succinct, and unambiguous communication. Using the "Six-Page Narrative" format in meetings is one of the distinctive features of Amazon's communication culture.

Employees compose in-depth narratives that are read aloud to all attendees at the start of meetings in place of PowerPoint presentations. By ensuring that all participants have a thorough understanding of the subject before the debate starts, this method promotes more knowledgeable and fruitful dialogues.

Additionally, another tactic to improve communication is Amazon's "Two-Pizza Team" rule, which states that teams should be small enough to be fed by two pizzas. More cohesive teamwork, speedier decision-making, and improved communication are all facilitated by smaller teams. Despite its enormous size, Amazon has been able to preserve its inventiveness and agility thanks to this strategy.

Mayo Clinic is a prime example of how good communication can improve teamwork and patient care in the healthcare industry. The foundation of the Mayo Clinic approach is an interdisciplinary communication and collaborative culture. In order to provide patients with the best treatment possible, doctors, nurses, and other healthcare workers collaborate closely and share information. Patients are guaranteed to receive thorough and well-coordinated care with this method.

Integrated electronic health records, or EHRs, are a vital part of Mayo Clinic's communication plan. EHRs make sure that everyone is on the same page by enabling real-time access to and updating of patient data by all team members. Frequent case conferences and team meetings improve communication even more, allowing medical professionals to discuss difficult cases and work together to create thorough treatment strategies. The excellent culture of communication at Mayo Clinic has greatly contributed to the hospital's stellar reputation for patient care.

Within the aviation industry, Southwest Airlines' success can be partially ascribed to its effective communication strategies. Southwest has fostered an environment that values candid communication and worker autonomy. The organization promotes a sense of ownership and teamwork by encouraging workers at all levels to share ideas and criticism.

Regular town hall meetings are a part of Southwest's communication strategy, where executives provide information and ask staff members for feedback. To keep everyone informed and engaged, the organization also makes use of a strong internal communication infrastructure. By placing a strong emphasis on communication, the organization can make sure that every employee is aware of its objectives and is motivated to work toward them. Southwest's excellent customer service and high staff morale are results of its emphasis on good communication.

Within the sports world, there are important lessons to be learned from the New England Patriots' communication techniques. The Patriots have established a direct and open communication culture under head coach Bill Belichick's direction. Belichick's coaching philosophy places a strong emphasis on making sure that every player is aware of their roles and responsibilities and that they are all in agreement with the team's goals.

Two essential facets of the Patriots' communication plan are team meetings and film sessions. Players get the chance to discuss strategies, evaluate their performance, and resolve any problems during these sessions. The team's disciplined and successful communication both on and off the field is a direct result of Belichick's emphasis on preparation and attention to detail. The Patriots' continued success in the NFL has been greatly attributed to this strategy.

In the business sector, Zappos serves as an example of how good communication affects customer service and company culture. Online shoe and apparel store Zappos is renowned for its dedication to providing outstanding customer service. A culture of open communication and openness supports this commitment.

At Zappos, open communication between staff members and management is encouraged. The company's open-door approach and flat organizational structure make it easy for staff members to voice issues and ideas. Additionally, Zappos values client feedback greatly and uses it to keep improving its goods and services. Through the cultivation of an efficient communication culture, Zappos has amassed a devoted clientele and a highly involved staff.

Within the field of education, the communication strategies employed by San Diego's High Tech High network of charter schools provide valuable perspectives on the significance of cooperation and openness. Teachers at High Tech High must collaborate closely in order to plan and carry out multidisciplinary projects as part of the school's project-based learning methodology. Regular team meetings and professional development workshops, when teachers exchange best practices and give feedback to one another, foster this collaborative culture.

Additionally, High Tech High stresses the value of communication between students and teachers. In order to foster an environment where students feel comfortable sharing their thoughts and asking questions, teachers try to create a welcoming and open classroom. This emphasis on communication promotes student engagement and achievement while also helping to create a healthy learning environment.

Effective communication is crucial in the creative industries, as demonstrated by the teamwork that made the television series "Game of Thrones" a success. David Benioff and D.B. Weiss, the show's creators, oversaw a sizable and diversified group of writers, directors, performers, and crew people. To ensure that everyone was in agreement with the show's vision and to coordinate the intricate production process, clear and consistent communication was crucial.

The intricate plotlines and several seasons of "Game of Thrones" were kept coherent and consistent by regular meetings, well-written scripts, and unambiguous orders. The creative team's capacity for excellent communication made it possible to adapt George R.R. Martin's epic narrative into one of the most critically acclaimed television shows ever.

The tale of the collaboration platform Slack serves as an example of how communication is critical to innovation and expansion in the tech company ecosystem. The company uses Slack's own product, which is intended to improve team communication, extensively to encourage staff collaboration. The seamless and effective flow of information throughout the company is ensured by channels, direct messaging, and integrated tools.

Slack's internal procedures demonstrate the company's dedication to openness and transparency. The management of the organization answers questions from staff members and provides updates during regular all-hands meetings. This culture of open communication promotes a sense of unity and purpose by keeping everyone informed and in sync. Slack's quick expansion and broad use can be largely attributed to its accomplishment in creating a cooperative and open work atmosphere.

Within the automotive sector, Toyota's communication strategies offer insightful information about the significance of ongoing development and information exchange. Effective communication at all levels is essential to Toyota's manufacturing system, which is renowned for its effectiveness and high caliber. Employees are encouraged to share suggestions for improving procedures and resolving issues as part of the company's "Kaizen" culture, which places an emphasis on continual improvement.

On the manufacturing floor, Toyota's use of visual management tools like Kanban boards promotes open and honest communication. Teams can monitor their progress, spot bottlenecks, and efficiently organize work with the aid of these technologies. Frequent brainstorming sessions and team meetings also improve communication and guarantee that problems are solved quickly and cooperatively. Toyota's reputation for quality and operational excellence is largely due to its dedication to effective communication.

Goldman Sachs's communication techniques in the financial sector serve as an example of how important clarity and transparency are in a high-stakes setting. Effective communication is highly valued at Goldman Sachs, both with clients and internally. The organization's "One Goldman Sachs" campaign encourages communication and cooperation throughout various departments and geographical areas.

Goldman Sachs makes use of a range of platforms and communication technologies to guarantee that information is shared safely and efficiently. Employees are kept informed about market trends, business performance, and strategic initiatives through regular meetings, reports, and updates. Goldman Sachs' emphasis on efficient communication helps it stay competitive and provide value to clients.

To sum up, a successful team's ability to communicate is essential to its success. We see that open, honest, and transparent communication promotes teamwork, creativity, and performance through real-world case studies of Pixar, Amazon, Mayo Clinic, Southwest Airlines, the New England Patriots, Zappos, High Tech High, "Game of Thrones," Slack, Toyota, and Goldman Sachs. These illustrations show how a deliberate approach to communication may improve team dynamics, increase productivity, and support sustained success. Leaders may foster an environment of successful communication that promotes both individual and group growth by establishing a culture where information is easily exchanged, ideas are discussed candidly, and criticism is highly appreciated.

CONFLICT RESOLUTION STRATEGIES

Any team dynamic will inevitably have conflict as a result of divergent viewpoints, objectives, and personalities. Effective conflict resolution, however, can turn disagreements into chances for development, creativity, and improved bonds between parties. This chapter explores a variety of conflict resolution techniques, supported by real-world case studies of businesses that have resolved disputes amicably to produce desirable results.

The method Microsoft, under Satya Nadella's leadership, has taken to resolving conflicts in a business setting is one of the most instructional instances available.

Microsoft was notorious for its internal rivalries and divided departments, which inhibited cooperation and creativity, when Nadella took over as CEO in 2014. Realizing that a shift in culture was required, Nadella ushered in a new philosophy that emphasized cooperation, empathy, and communication.

Nadella provided forums for staff members to voice their opinions and concerns and promoted candid communication. He underlined the value of understanding and listening to diverse points of view, which aided in tearing down barriers across teams. Organizing frequent "CEO Connection" meetings, where staff members could address issues with management directly, was one of Nadella's major initiatives. This openness and readiness to confront problems head-on promoted a more welcoming and collaborative atmosphere.

The creation of the Surface tablet was one significant Microsoft dispute resolution achievement. At first, there was a big dispute on the product's direction between the software and hardware teams. Nadella encouraged candid conversations in which members of both teams shared their hopes and worries. The teams eventually came to an understanding by concentrating on common objectives and promoting respect for one another. This allowed for the successful launch of the Surface line, which has since grown to be a significant offering for Microsoft.

Another interesting case study in the realm of internet startups is the tale of Airbnb. When it first launched in 2008, Airbnb had serious internal strife as it expanded quickly. Tensions arose because the founders, Brian Chesky, Joe Gebbia, and Nathan Blecharczyk, had conflicting goals and management philosophies. The founders hired an executive coach to help them with these problems, and the coach helped them become better communicators and resolve conflicts.

The coach taught strategies like active listening, in which each founder would hear out the other person's viewpoint completely before answering. They also learnt how to communicate honestly about their worries and emotions without blaming others or becoming defensive. Their leadership team became stronger and more unified as a result of this exercise. Because of this, Airbnb was able to get through its early growth challenges and become a major force in the hotel sector.

Because of its team-based approach to patient care, the Mayo Clinic provides a model for dispute resolution in the healthcare industry. To deliver complete care, interdisciplinary teams of physicians, nurses, and other healthcare workers collaborate at the Mayo Clinic.

Conflicts may arise from this collaborative paradigm because different people may have different ideas about how to manage patients and create treatment plans.

The Mayo Clinic has put in place formalized conflict resolution procedures to handle these disputes. All team members can express their opinions in an open discussion and debate environment that is provided by regular team meetings. The clinic also stresses the value of a patient-centered strategy, in which the patient's best interests are the first priority. Mayo Clinic successfully handles disagreements and guarantees excellent patient care by concentrating on shared objectives and keeping lines of communication open.

Effective dispute resolution in sports is best shown by the Chicago Bulls under coach Phil Jackson in the 1990s. Internal disputes plagued the club under Michael Jordan's leadership, especially between Jordan and other important players like Dennis Rodman and Scottie Pippen. Jackson, who was well-known for his distinctive coaching approach, promoted harmony and settled disputes by applying ideas from Native American and Zen Buddhism.

Jackson urged players to participate in open dialogue sessions and mindfulness exercises so they could voice their worries and frustrations in a nonjudgmental setting.

The participants' regard and understanding for one another increased as a result of this strategy. In order to promote a sense of team responsibility, Jackson also underlined the significance of each player's role and contribution to the team's success. It was thanks in large part to this conflict resolution technique that the Bulls won six NBA titles in that particular timeframe.

The Gates Foundation's approach to conflict resolution offers important lessons for the nonprofit sector. It was inevitable that disagreements would arise in a diverse team working on complicated global challenges. In order to resolve these disputes, the foundation supported an inclusive and respectful culture. In order to give staff members the skills they needed to resolve conflicts amicably, regular workshops and training sessions on these topics were held.

The organization also established a peer mediation program in which qualified staff members served as mediators to assist in resolving disputes among coworkers. This program promoted candid communication and teamwork, which aided in speedy dispute resolution and the preservation of a pleasant work atmosphere. The Gates Foundation's dedication to constructive dispute resolution has allowed them to work with a motivated and cohesive workforce to address some of the most important issues facing the globe.

Starbucks provides a case study in proactive conflict resolution for the retail sector. Starbucks has prioritized open communication and employee satisfaction under Howard Schultz's direction. The idea of "Partner Open Forums," which Schultz created, allowed staff members—referred to as partners—to communicate their ideas and grievances with upper management.

These discussion boards gave staff members a place to express their ideas and feel heard, which promoted an open and trustworthy environment. Schultz also made sure managers had the abilities to resolve conflicts by implementing conflict resolution training. Starbucks has been able to preserve a positive workplace culture and high levels of employee engagement thanks to its proactive approach to conflict resolution.

The entertainment industry presented a number of obstacles and disputes throughout Peter Jackson's "The Lord of the Rings" film trilogy's production. The production had a huge budget, a large cast and crew, intricate logistics, and intense financial strain. Schedules for production, budget allocation, and artistic differences all became points of contention.

In order to resolve these disputes, Peter Jackson promoted an atmosphere that was inclusive and

217

cooperative. He met on a regular basis with important team members to work through problems together and have frank conversations. Jackson also promoted an environment where people respected and valued one another's efforts. This method produced one of the most successful film trilogies in movie history by resolving disputes and keeping the project on schedule.

Toyota's organizational culture is ingrained with a dispute resolution strategy unique to the automobile industry. Effective conflict resolution is part of the Toyota Production System's emphasis on respect for people and ongoing improvement. Toyota has a technique for resolving disputes on the manufacturing floor called "A3" thinking. This approach entails recording the issue, determining its underlying cause, and working together to create a solution.

Since all employees participate in identifying and addressing issues, the A3 method promotes open communication and teamwork. Toyota's conflict resolution strategy reduces misconceptions and fosters productive communication by emphasizing facts and data over subjective opinions. Toyota's reputation for excellence and productivity has been largely attributed to this approach.

Goldman Sachs' approach to conflict resolution in the financial sector emphasizes the value of communication and transparency in high-stakes situations. Mutual respect and straightforward, unambiguous communication are highly valued at the company. Employees at Goldman Sachs receive frequent performance assessments with constructive criticism as part of an organized feedback process.

By promoting open communication between managers and staff, this feedback approach helps resolve issues before they become more serious. Additionally, Goldman Sachs offers training in communication and conflict resolution techniques to make sure that staff members are prepared to handle conflicts in a professional manner. This proactive approach to dispute resolution contributes to the upkeep of a productive and cooperative workplace.

The International Baccalaureate (IB) program's dispute resolution techniques provide insightful insights for the education sector. The International Baccalaureate program (IB) is a global education initiative that prioritizes the enhancement of students' interpersonal and conflict resolution abilities. IB schools educate students conflict resolution skills like negotiation, mediation, and active listening as part of their curricula.

By giving pupils these abilities, the IB program promotes a respectful and cooperative atmosphere. Regular workshops and role-playing activities in schools enable students learn conflict resolution and use these abilities in practical settings. Students who get this emphasis on conflict resolution education will be better equipped to manage conflict in the classroom and in their future employment.

VitalSmarts, a company that specializes in organizational performance, offers a convincing example of effective dispute resolution tactics in the context of corporate training. VitalSmarts provides training courses like "Crucial Conversations" and "Crucial Accountability," which educate people on how to manage difficult conversations and find effective solutions to problems.

Finding common ground, remaining composed under pressure, and active listening are among the abilities that are emphasized in the program. VitalSmarts helps individuals practice these abilities in a secure setting by using case studies and role-playing exercises. After putting VitalSmarts' training into practice, organizations saw notable gains in dispute resolution and communication, which improved team dynamics and output.

The New York City Fire Department (FDNY) offers insightful approaches to dispute resolution in the sphere of public service. The FDNY frequently encounters disagreements because of its diverse personnel and demanding work environment. The department has put in place a thorough conflict resolution program that consists of support services, mediation, and training.

The training curriculum of the FDNY has a strong emphasis on interpersonal, negotiation, and cultural competence abilities. Peer mediation is another service the department offers, in which professionally trained firemen serve as mediators to assist in resolving disputes amongst their coworkers. This program fosters an environment of respect and understanding between participants, which supports the upkeep of a cohesive and productive team.

In conclusion, any organization's ability to successfully resolve conflicts is critical to its long-term viability. Constructive communication, mutual respect, and a focus on shared goals are essential for resolving conflicts, as demonstrated by the following real-world case studies: Microsoft, Airbnb, Mayo Clinic, Chicago Bulls, Gates Foundation, Starbucks, "The Lord of the Rings" film production, Toyota, Goldman Sachs, International Baccalaureate program, VitalSmarts, and the New York City Fire Department. These illustrations show how a systematic approach to conflict resolution may turn disagreements into chances for development, creativity, and improved bonds between parties. Through establishing a setting that encourages candid and productive dispute resolution, leaders may cultivate a cooperative and upbeat team culture that promotes both individual and group achievement.

Conclusion

Now that we have completed our investigation into the topics of mindset, organizational dynamics, and leadership, it is clear that achieving mastery over these areas is a challenging yet worthwhile path. Every chapter has examined crucial elements that, when combined, form a potent foundation for development on both a personal and professional level. The goal of this book is to give you a thorough understanding and useful insights into cultivating an exceptional leadership style and next-level business attitude.

The foundation was established in the first chapter, which explored the idea of a business mindset. It examined how managing the intricacies of contemporary business environments requires a growth-oriented approach. A business mindset emphasizes flexibility, resilience, and a never-ending search for progress, going beyond simple technical understanding. It is the prism through which obstacles are seen as chances and setbacks as stepping stones toward achievement. This way of thinking is dynamic and changes with experience and education. It forms the basis for all the leadership attributes covered in later chapters.

The focus moved to the fundamentals of leadership in the second chapter. What qualities distinguish a leader?

Key leadership attributes were examined in order to answer this question. Being an effective leader involves more than just exercising power; it also involves motivating and directing others toward a common goal. Emotional intelligence, communication prowess, decisiveness, and the capacity to build team trust and collaboration are all characteristics of true leaders. These attributes can be developed via self-awareness, deliberate practice, and a dedication to one's own development; they are not innate.

The differentiation between management and leadership was yet another important subject examined in this chapter. Leadership is about inspiring, motivating, and influencing change, whereas management is about procedures, effectiveness, and holding things under control. While both positions are vital, they call for distinct skill sets and attitudes. Successful leaders frequently wear two hats, striking a balance between the managerial duties and the inspiring and visionary responsibilities of leadership. Maintaining a dynamic and adaptable organization that can survive in a world that is changing quickly requires this duality.

The third chapter examined the complex and important function of emotional intelligence in leadership. Social skills, empathy, self-control, and self-awareness are all included in emotional intelligence, or EQ. Leaders with high EQ are skilled at reading both their own and others' emotions, which helps them deal with interpersonal situations well. In this chapter, it was discussed how emotional intelligence sets leaders apart and improves their performance, especially when it comes to creating cohesive teams and a positive workplace culture.

We looked closely at communication abilities, which are yet another essential component of successful leadership. In order to resolve disagreements, build a transparent and trusting culture, and align team members with organizational goals, clear, succinct, and sympathetic communication is crucial. Effective communicators are able to express their vision, offer helpful criticism, and engage in active listening to their team members. This fosters an atmosphere that fosters innovation and improves teamwork, propelling the company toward success.

We then looked at two more essential competencies: problem-solving and decision-making. Leaders frequently have to make difficult decisions with significant consequences that call for a combination of critical thinking, gut instinct, and in-depth situational knowledge. Gathering pertinent data, analyzing options, taking long-term effects into account, and maintaining flexibility in the face of shifting conditions are all necessary for making effective decisions. On the other hand, problem-solving necessitates a methodical approach in order to pinpoint underlying issues, provide workarounds, and successfully execute adjustments. These abilities are essential for managing the risks and difficulties that come with leadership positions.

Another essential component of leadership, presence and confidence building, was covered in great detail. A leader who exudes confidence is able to inspire and encourage their team because it gives them credibility and trust. The capacity to command attention and exude power through one's demeanor, tone of voice, and body language is known as presence, or the "it" factor. These qualities can be acquired via introspection, training, and a dedication to ongoing development. Leaders that exude confidence and presence are more capable of setting a good example, making a positive influence, and propelling their businesses ahead.

In Chapter 4, the idea of setting an example was discussed, emphasizing the value of honesty, sincerity, and responsibility. Leaders who provide a strong example for their team members by modeling the attitudes and actions they want to see in them. Setting a positive example for others to follow encourages a climate of mutual respect and trust. Case studies from real life situations demonstrated how executives who lead by example have a beneficial knock-on effect that affects the culture of the entire company and promotes long-term success.

Another important issue that emphasized the importance of strategic thinking and foresight in leadership was developing a vision and mission. While a mission statement clearly outlines the firm's basic beliefs and objectives, a captivating vision statement gives the organization direction and purpose. Effective communicators of vision and mission may unite their people behind a common goal, encouraging dedication and alignment. To prioritize tasks, make decisions, and stay focused in the face of conflicting demands, strategic clarity is crucial.

The capacity to uplift and encourage others was thoroughly examined, emphasizing the significance of identifying and utilizing personal assets, offering significant acknowledgment, and cultivating a feeling of inclusion. Positive and effective work environments are created by leaders that inspire and motivate their teams, making everyone feel appreciated and included. This chapter demonstrated how motivation encompasses factors like personal development, autonomy, and a feeling of purpose in addition to financial incentives.

Through real-world examples, the critical components of effective leadership—delegation and empowerment—

were examined. By assigning duties and responsibilities to team members, leaders may concentrate on strategic priorities. Conversely, empowerment is giving team members the tools, encouragement, and independence they need to be successful. A culture of trust and accountability is fostered by leaders who are skilled at empowerment and delegation, which inspires people to accept responsibility for their actions and make a positive impact on the organization.

The habits of highly successful people were examined in Chapter 5, which showed how dependable routines like goal-setting, time management, and ongoing learning support long-term success. Successful people's real-world case studies emphasized the value of self-control, tenacity, and a growth attitude in reaching both personal and professional objectives. When deliberately developed, these behaviors lay the groundwork for long-term success and contentment.

A thorough analysis of time management and productivity was conducted, with a focus on the importance of planning, attention, and priority in achieving maximum efficiency. Effective time managers are able to maintain a healthy work-life balance, prevent burnout, and foster a positive work atmosphere. This chapter offered doable methods for improving productivity and time management, empowering leaders to accomplish their objectives and provide their people with the help they need.

Another important subject was the value of resilience and adaptation, emphasizing how leaders face obstacles head-on and take initiative. Adaptability is the ability to change with the times, whereas resilience is the ability to overcome hardship. These traits are exhibited by resilient and innovative leaders who provide an environment where teams are free to try new things, fail forward with learning, and adapt to change.

The topic of ongoing education and development was brought up in relation to individual and corporate development. Continuously learning leaders improve their abilities, remain ahead of market trends, and cultivate an innovative culture. This chapter provided examples of how a dedication to lifelong learning propels achievement over time and helps leaders negotiate the challenges of a world that is changing quickly.

The dynamics of team formation, such as selecting the proper candidates, creating a supportive team environment, and facilitating efficient team communication, were covered in Chapter 6. Finding individuals who share the organization's values and have the required abilities and qualities is part of the recruitment process. In order to cultivate a positive team culture, one must provide a setting where people are appreciated, engaged, and valued. As will be covered in-depth, successful team communication is critical to cooperation, resolving conflicts, and accomplishing group objectives.

Real-world case studies were used in these chapters to give readers specific examples of how these ideas are put to use in a variety of situations, including startups, business environments, sports, healthcare, and education. These case studies demonstrate how effective communication, emotional intelligence, strategic thinking, and continuous improvement are globally relevant concepts, even though the details of leadership and organizational dynamics may differ throughout industries.

In summary, cultivating excellent leadership abilities and acquiring a next-level business mindset are complex processes that call for practice, intention, and a dedication to both personal and professional development. You can lead your team to sustained success, inspire and encourage them, and negotiate the challenges of today's complex business environments by adopting the concepts and tactics covered in this book. As you proceed on this road, keep in mind that becoming a leader is a continuous process that requires learning, adapting, and growing.

www.ingramcontent.com/pod-product-compliance
Lightning Source LLC
Chambersburg PA
CBHW071915210526
45479CB00002B/425